DIVINE H.

DELIVERANCE

AND

THE KINGDOM OF GOD

by

Rev Trevor Dearing MA BD

International Preacher, Retired Church of England
Clergyman, Minister of Divine Healing

[handwritten inscription] Man 3/6/2020

To Charles

Best Wishes

Love in Jesus

Published by Crossbridge Books
Worcester
www.crossbridgeeducational.com

© Crossbridge Books 2020

All rights reserved. No part of this publication
may be reproduced, stored in a retrieval system,
or transmitted in any form or by any means –
electronic, mechanical, photocopying, recording
or otherwise – without prior permission of the
Copyright owner.

ISBN 978 0 9569089 7 1

British Library Cataloguing in Publication Data
A catalogue record for this book is available from the British Library

*All proceeds from the sale of this book will be used to further the
mission of Crossbridge Books to publish Christian books.*

Also published by Crossbridge Books:

TOTAL HEALING by Trevor Dearing

GOD AND HEALING OF THE MIND
by Trevor Dearing

**MEDITATE AND BE MADE WHOLE THROUGH
JESUS CHRIST** by Trevor Dearing

IT'S TRUE by Trevor Dearing

THE LIVING WORD (daily readings from the psalms)
by Trevor Dearing

THE GOD OF MIRACLES by Trevor and Anne Dearing

CALLED TO BE A WIFE by Anne Dearing

ACKNOWLEDGEMENTS

This book is dedicated to the memory of my late wife Anne and my four Christian sibling children Philip, Ruth, Rachel and Rebecca with my love and gratitude.

I wish to give heartfelt thanks to Ruth Price-Mohr, and Crossbridge Books, for her very painstaking and hard work on this book and being so very helpful with my failing eyesight. I am so very grateful to Eileen Mohr's fellowship and help over many years.

Thanks also to Mrs Elizabeth Young for her great support and encouragement in many years of ministry. I have also been greatly helped by Miss Abigail Reynolds and Charles Cartwright in reading through the manuscript.

I also wish to thank my son-in-law Richard Izzard for designing the cover.

CONTENTS   *Page*

INTRODUCTION

I am writing this as an Anglican clergyman, now retired and at the age of eighty-six. I had been married for fifty-seven years until my wife went suddenly to Glory on the first of December 2014. Until then she had been a wonderful partner in my ministry. I have been engaged in the ministry of divine healing and also in the ministry of evangelism as well as pastoral care, since I was converted from atheism at the age of nineteen, firstly into Methodism and then being ordained as a curate and eventually a priest in the Church of England. I began laying hands on the sick at St Paul's Church, Hainault, Arrowsmith Road, Chigwell, Essex, a small rather prefabricated building, as it was built after the war, in September 1970. I had become the new vicar of the parish and was met by a small number of traditional Anglicans used to traditional services. They had, however, made an incursion into a healing ministry through the teaching of the Rev Roy Jeremias of the London Healing Mission, but had hardly begun to practice this wonderful ministry when I arrived.

I have written books on divine healing as well as taken hundreds of services involving this ministry to thousands of people in England and all over the world. I have written books on this subject, the main one on this subject being 'Total Healing' which involves the healing of the body, the mind and the spirit. I have also read works on the subject written by others, but what I have to say is that these books, including mine, have always been about divine healing only as if it was a ministry all on its own, and they have not related the ministry in any way to evangelism and the Christian Gospel.

Similarly, books I have read about mission and evangelism, and preaching the Gospel, which I have always done, were solely about that subject, and included nothing about divine healing or the relationship between divine healing and the Christian Gospel as an inseparable whole to be practiced together as a combined ministry, as was so in the ministry of our Lord Jesus Christ and the apostles as recorded in the Acts of the Apostles. I hope to set this dichotomy right by showing both Biblically and in practice, the relevance of these two commands of our Lord Jesus Christ, as he sent his apostles out in mission and to further His work saying "Preach the Gospel, heal the sick and cast out demons"[1]. This is what they did in total obedience to Him, doing his Christian work altogether as Jesus commanded, and as seen in their ministry in the Acts of the Apostles.

I am going to expound the relationship between divine healing and the Christian Gospel as an inseparable whole in the teaching and ministry of our Lord Jesus Christ and the early apostles.

We have now reached the point where we have said that the proclamation of the Christian Gospel and divine healing are usually dealt with in Christian literature, and in Christian services, as separate entities each in themselves, but this also should not exclude the commission of Jesus also to cast out demons which He ordered His disciples to do[2], and they came back to Him saying 'even the demons are subject to us in your name', and He said 'rejoice not in this, but that your names are written in Heaven'[3]. So in a study of this kind, dealing with the Christian proclamation of His message, directed by Jesus, and continued after His resurrection in the Acts of the Apostles, we find that not only did the disciples cast out demons but that also this ministry was often used in the Christian ministry in the Acts of the Apostles, and talked about in the epistles[4] of the apostles. I have not dealt with this so far because I see it in Scripture as a way of healing. Jesus' ministry of deliverance always resulted in either physical healing, when a demon was cast out, or in the ceasing of mental torment or emotional problems, and the person being at peace in their mind.

So this particular ministry, of what I prefer to call 'deliverance', or what usually is called by secular people 'exorcism', was a definite commission of Jesus that His disciples had to follow, in casting out these tormenting, evil, debilitating, and often sickness-causing evil spirits. So we shall deal with them in our study as part of the fact that the proclamation of the Gospel of Jesus and His Kingdom, and divine healing in His name, and deliverance from evil spirits by His power, was an intrinsic whole in the Christian commission in its early days. I will be showing that this commission

3

should be fulfilled in today's ministry of the church as it engages with a secular and evil world in its environment. So the full proclamation of Jesus to His disciples to preach the Gospel, heal the sick and cast out demons, is as important a mission of the church today as it was in Bible days.

Jesus' commission to His disciples to go out on their first missionary expedition was a three-fold command to preach the Gospel, heal the sick and cast out demons[5]. We have seen that the first two ministries have been treated very much as entities in their own right, rather than in any particular deliberate relationship, on the part of Jesus and the understanding of the apostles. Now we turn to the third part of His command which was to cast out demons. This again was something which He had Himself done through His powerful spoken word[6] to these evil forces occupying human lives, and He now wished the disciples to embark on the same task. Where demons come from, or came from, in the time of the New Testament we are not told. Certainly they are seen as evil, and with ways of inhabiting and affecting human beings badly in their bodies, with sickness and infirmity, and in their minds with some sort of confusion[7], or indeed torment. Their leader seems to be Satan, in his ways of harming human beings, or taking residence in their lives, or as Jesus once called him Beelzebub the prince of the demons. Demons are not the only evil spirits encountered in the New Testament and dealt with by Jesus, there were also unclean spirits[8].

So the disciples of Jesus went on their way to do this wonderful 'threefold work'. They set out as ordinary human beings but with the command of Jesus to extend His Kingdom by preaching the Gospel, and healing the sick, and casting out evil spirits.

PART ONE

The gracious calling of the Lord

Chapter 1

My call to preach the Gospel

I could not have looked less a prospective preacher of the Gospel, than when once again I excused myself from the 9 o'clock Epilogue at the Queen's Hall Church Youth Club which I attended regularly on a Tuesday and a Thursday. This Epilogue, consisting of a hymn, a Bible reading and a prayer, was taken by Sister Elizabeth Gillings, a Deaconess of the Methodist Church. It didn't last very long, but it was too much religion for me at that stage of my life when I had had no religious upbringing at home whatsoever; Jesus was never mentioned in our house, and the reality of God was never discussed. I was not used to anything to do with religion, and in fact I didn't like anything to do with it. As I thought my way through things in my mind, I decided there was no God at all because of the suffering in the world which a loving good God would not allow, and so we had to get on as human beings, living as best we could, making use of such aids as came our way, and such entertainment, like table tennis, which we enjoyed.

However, I was not a very healthy seventeen-year-old when I went to the youth club or tried to go to work. At the age of eleven, I had already had my first terrible panic attack, and this was the beginning of a long period, eight years in fact, of terrible mental disorder. These included emotional fears, anxiety, depression, panic, racing heart, trembling legs, sweat-with-fear, inability to sleep, and phobias, which I had endured for eight years but tried hard not to show to anybody else, especially the young people at the youth club. Also, I was extremely thin in build although I was tall, and I was covered with very ferocious and large acne spots all over my face, that leaked a lot of yellow liquid, and they went down my back and stomach as well. I was very uncomfortable, didn't look at all nice and presentable to any young lady, and I felt a bit of an outcast, although the young people welcomed me and tried to make me feel at home. I knew I was a sick and almost disfigured young man.

However, after I had been going to the youth club for several months, and I was at that particular age, my eyes fell on a very lovely young lady who seemed to give me quite a lot of attention, and I felt I would like to get to know her and be her friend. So I made an approach to her along those lines and she said I could walk her home if I attended the Sunday evening service at the Queen's Hall Church Mission and listened to the sermon. And so I thought well one hour of religion will do me no harm; one hour of boredom I can stand, especially to take this young lady home and maybe become a special friend. So there came the evening when at 6.30 I met her at the door of the church and sat down, very uncomfortably on the back row of the church next to her, and decided to do my best to understand what was going on in the service. I did not know any of the hymns, I did not know when to stand up or sit down. I buried my head in my hands and closed my eyes and let my mind wander during the prayers and Bible readings. But when the sermon came around, I found the Rev William D Watts a fine orator; he could preach and speak very well, and I was pleased that he did not usually take Bible passages or texts for his messages but common themes and secular themes from the world around us. I remember him once preaching at that particular time on the theme 'The Cruel Sea' which was showing at the cinemas.

I attended this evening's service to get to know the young lady better and sat there feeling anxious and ill, an illness, as I have said, from which I suffered badly. However, one Sunday evening, Reverend Watts took a Bible text as his theme. It was Jesus saying "Come unto me all you who are weary and heavy laden and I will give you rest. Take my yoke upon you and learn of me, for I am meek and lowly in heart and you will find rest for your souls, for my yoke is easy and my burden is light"[9]. I did not remember all that scripture at the time, but the word 'rest' struck home to me because I did not know rest in my mind or in my body, so I just whispered, half aloud, "Jesus Christ if you really are alive please help me because I think I will die before I am twenty-five years of age". As I said these words, suddenly what I recognised vaguely as a great peace, wonderful peace, filled my mind, and my body was feeling very strange; I felt a comfortable warmth, and I began to feel really well.

The most important thing of all though was that this person Jesus, who lived 2,000 years ago, really became contemporary to me in my need and I knew He was going to give me rest and peace and make me well. So after that service and taking the young lady home, I knelt by my bedside and said "Jesus, forgive me all my sins and take my life into your service".

I continued at the youth club for a few weeks after this when a strange thing happened. I had been thinking in my mind 'wouldn't it be wonderful if I could share some thoughts about my new-found-faith with a congregation' as what I understood to be a preacher, but I used to cast these thoughts aside as nonsense because I did not know any of the Bible or very much at all about Christianity. However, one Thursday evening, in the middle of a game of table tennis, Sister Elizabeth Gillings came up to me, stopped the game, I lost the point, and she said, "Trevor, have you ever felt you ought to be a preacher?" I nearly collapsed with shock. I stopped playing table tennis and sat with her and said, "Yes I have, but isn't it stupid because I haven't been a Christian for more than a few weeks; I don't even know the Bible." She said, "Well you'll undergo some training. Mr Watts and I have felt that you are called to be a preacher from the very first time we ever saw you." So I began to embark on Bible study exercises and tests, and because I could not really pronounce my 'r's or my 'l's when I was speaking, I decided I would pay for some private elocution lessons that cured this defect in my speech. I also learnt from this elocutionist, who was a Christian, how to throw my voice to the back of a room.

Eventually the time came round when I was going to preach my first sermon at a very small church with a small congregation; it was my first attempt at doing so. I wrote the sermon out in long hand and passed my thoughts to Mr Watts who said, "I'm sorry Trevor, this is all a rambling discourse which will not be followed by anybody, I must ask you to try again." So I did. This time I decided to break my message up into points, and I chose something I'd seen in the Bible in a book which I did not know called Joshua, and the theme was the sin of a man called Achan[10] which caused the Israelite people to lose the battle and flee before their enemies. I again wrote this out in full. Mr Watts was pleased with this, saying it was much better than the first attempt, and he advised me to preach it reading it aloud into a mirror. This I did. The first time I did it, it lasted 20 minutes, but I thought next time 10 minutes, next time 5 minutes, and the next time, when I preached it at the church, it was just 5 minutes long. The congregation were expecting something longer than this in time so their service had finished early, so they decided to have cups of tea and a good chat, and a good time was had by all. I was relieved that I had at least preached once.

I began to preach like this now and again and I also took a weekly periodical to learn about Methodism called the Methodist Recorder. In this one week I saw an advertisement that attracted my attention, 'Young men training to preach and wanting to be evangelists, why not come and study at Cliff College in Derbyshire with others like you and learn your faith and ministry, and train to be an evangelist'. Apparently you could go there at that time without paying any money whatsoever in fees, and I wrote to the Principal. Mr Watts backed my application and I was accepted to go to Cliff College in the September after my twentieth birthday.

When I arrived there, I was disappointed because I had seen on their brochure that a lot of sport was played at the college, including table tennis and cricket, but I found in fact that most of the time was spent doing Bible lessons and having lecturers teaching the Bible. So I got to know my Bible really well. I took my local preacher's examinations, which I passed with honours. They found I was a very intelligent young man, as I had proved when I had been able to attend school, by passing my school certificate with matriculation exemption. So I studied and preached at Cliff College. I went out to preach from there, and eventually we went on what was called a trek. This was six or seven of us going under a leader. Most of the students had to push their carts containing their clothes, books and many other things along roads leading to seaside resorts where they would preach, but I, because I was still seen to be rather a weak young man, was elected to go on the much further mission and put in a minibus with the leader called Joe Douglas. When we arrived there, I found I was not asked to preach very often, only very rarely, because I was so new to it. But one day Joe Douglas said to me "I have a special mission for you Trevor; I want you to go and see an elderly lady who is dying of cancer, and she especially wants to see a person named Trevor Dearing. Will you go tomorrow morning?" So I opened the little gate at the end of a long footpath leading to her front door and knocked. I heard a feeble voice say "Come in," and I went in, and there at the end of the room was an old lady lying in bed, obviously very frail and weak. She had scripture texts printed all around the walls of her little room. "Come here," she said, "and kneel by the side of my bed," which I did, not knowing what was going to happen. She then reached out her feeble left hand from the bed, put it on my head and said, "Young man, the Lord has shown me that you, particularly you, who I wanted to see, are going to be used for the winning of thousands and the healing of hundreds." With that she put her head back and died. I was shattered and confused. I found my trek leader Joe and attended the funeral, and then we went on with our trek mission.

The trek in the mini bus took us to Newcastle and to preach at a church there; a very large mission church called Prudhoe Street Methodist Mission. Joe Douglas had been reluctant to allow me to preach because of my so-called modernist liberal views of the Bible, but he saw I was a sincere Christian in our journeys and decided to let me preach at this concluding service of our trek. Prudhoe Street Mission was a very large building, and on the night that I preached it was absolutely packed, with at least two hundred people. I preached a sermon that I had been thinking about for some time on Jesus' words on the cross, "It is finished."[11] I preached on the fact that because Jesus had given His life completely – and the words 'it is finished' meant completed – so we could have a new life, saying to Him 'it is finished'; starting our new life in Him. After I had preached the sermon, I did what I had been taught to do at Cliff College, I asked people who wanted to accept Jesus as Saviour and Lord to come and kneel at the communion rail. Well everyone there was a Christian I am sure but I was surprised when out of the crowd came a man who was dirty, dishevelled, unshaven, with matted hair, and clothes dropping into rags. He was obviously a man who had slept on the streets, who lived on the streets, and was what we would call in those days a tramp. He slowly made his way forward down the aisle, knelt at the communion rail and cried many tears for a long time, and then I prayed over him and he went to be counselled by one of our leaders.

The next day I saw him after a breakfast provided by the Mission, washed, shaved, dressed in new clothes given him by a member of Prudhoe Street Mission; a clean man singing 'Blessed assurance, Jesus is mine' going out for his first day's work. I praised the Lord that He had called me to preach and be an evangelist even if just for that one man. That was a wonderful person coming to Christ, my first real convert in my whole ministry, as I became sure I had been called by God to be an evangelist.

I ought really to add something wonderful that happened to me at Cliff College whilst I was there, which deepened my faith, brought me into a very close communion with God which I have still maintained, and was a turning point in my Christian life, reaching real depths of spirituality and love for God.

This was a special service conducted in Calver Parish Church, a small Anglican church, by Cliff College marking their fiftieth anniversary of the existence of this colleges' mission. The church was packed. I had to attend, but my bags were packed because I felt I was such an unhappy person at Cliff College, with my rather liberal views of the Bible, that I would have to go home. I couldn't really stay feeling so unhappy. The service went on and the Rev Maurice Barnett, the visiting preacher from London, preached on a subject I had never heard before. It was all about living a sacrificial life for Jesus[12]; about giving your life entirely to Him; laying your life on the altar; abandoning your life to Him in its entirety whether you were rich or poor, lived long or short lives, sick or healthy, married or single; whatever happened you were totally abandoned in your whole being to the person of Jesus and to His work. He did use that word abandoned very frequently. I knew I hadn't abandoned my life to Jesus. I felt as if I had never heard anything like this before; he said, "You have never heard anything like it before". I thought 'I'll have to do something'; he said, "You'll have to do something". I thought 'I'll have to run through the door'. He picked up every thought I had; he said, "Don't run through the door, run down here and abandon your life to the Lord Jesus Christ". I didn't look to see if anybody else was going, I didn't run through the door, I ran down that little church, knelt at the communion rail, the only one there, and amidst many tears abandoned my life; Jesus got all there was of Trevor Dearing for the rest of his life.

The peace which followed this dedication of my life, full surrender, was profound, and my experience of God rich and deep; my determination to serve Him whatever the cost now given new enhancement and I stayed at Cliff College, writing to Mr Watts the minister 'don't worry about me I've joined them'. This was a profound experience. I still maintain that attitude of abandonment at the age of eighty-six. It has been the hallmark, the whole essence, of my Christianity.

But God is no one's debtor, a few weeks later at a youth convention at the college I was serving tea, as one of the students, out of an aluminium pot, going around those who had come to the convention – young people – pouring tea into their cups, when I came across one young lady I had never seen before. I stopped and looked at her and I felt a strange warmth in my heart; I felt I loved her and I had never even spoken to her. I knew I had to marry her if I possibly could; I felt even God wanted it. I went on, and after I had finished serving the teas I went out, and this young woman quickly ran out after me even though I didn't know her. She said, "I've been told your name is Trevor Dearing, and Trevor I don't know you but I feel in my heart that God is saying I have to marry you." It was a marriage made in Heaven lasting fifty-seven years. After three years engagement, we married in the Methodist Church in Stamford where Anne lived.

So I left Cliff College and the Home Mission Department of the Methodist Church asked me if I would go and look after ten churches for a year in a very rural place in Norfolk, where there were little villages with little churches. I agreed to do so, on very little pay. I would look after ten of these churches, and on a Sunday cycle twenty miles, often in pitch black darkness with a little lamp on my bike, and preach in three churches; preach three times. Besides the ten churches under my care, I did the youth work in the churches, started a Christian Endeavour group in my main church, and tried my hardest to do Christian work as a young pastor. I had pastoral problems to deal with, like two stalwart women, Christians who wouldn't speak to each other but came into church through different doors; sorting things out like that; a layman who was having an affair with a preacher in the church. So it was a learning period for me, and a difficult time.

Eventually, I was accepted to be a minister of the Methodist Church and had to go to Leeds Theological College to train to be a minister and do my Bible studies. In that place I came top of all the candidates for the ministry around the country and won a prize for being top in exegesis of the New Testament and New Testament Greek. It would seem that I was an intelligent and deep thinking human. I wrote my first book, 'Wesleyan and Tractarian worship', describing the true deep Christian movements of John Wesley, and John Henry Newman, who had formed a Holy Club at Oxford before his ordination. In his diary, John Wesley wrote, on May 24th 1738, "My heart was strangely warmed and I felt I did trust in Christ".

So I went out as a curate and a vicar, convinced that God had called me to full-time service, to be a preacher of the Gospel. I went out into the Methodist Circuit in Brighouse in Yorkshire. It was during this time that I felt drawn to the Anglican Church. I hadn't been brought up a Methodist, and loved the Church of England and its sacramental life. I got to know the Anglican vicar John Lister very closely. I became very involved in his church - early morning sacraments - and eventually felt I had really grown to be an Anglican.

At Wesley Theological College in Leeds I obtained a Bachelor of Divinity degree and later went to Birmingham University where I obtained a Masters of Theology. My education was growing deeper. I was ordained as an Anglican clergyman and went out to preach in my first curacies and Parish and saw God really at work in them although I preached theological tomes and lectures, and not really the

Gospel because this is where I had come to in my education and thinking. But certainly it had been proved that I had been called to be a preacher. I felt this was confirmed while I was in one of those Colleges in Leeds, preaching on a Sunday evening in a Methodist church. I again, like at Prudhoe Street Mission, made a call for people to accept Christ because Jesus came to seek and to save that which is lost, and a young man named Derek Thackeray responded and knelt at the communion rail. Anne and I invited him round to our little place for tea; we taught him a lot about the faith. He has kept in communication with me all these years, phoning me only last week, an unmarried man, to say I had years and years ago set him on the right path and he had been awarded an MBE.

I became a vicar in Barnsley, but somehow in all this, as time passed, with married life and children, although I was still a keen Christian, something of the fire of Cliff College had died in me. I was preaching but now more theological lectures; having deep devotions in my own private time. I eventually was called to be vicar of St Paul's church Hainault where things really took off; I preached the Gospel and hundreds were won for the Kingdom of God. Trevor Dearing called to preach the Gospel.

Chapter 2

Called to heal the sick

When the crowd of nearly 600 people attending our Gospel healing service at St Paul's Church Hainault on a Tuesday evening saw me, the vicar, walk across the church and take hold of a young woman's hand who was sitting in a wheelchair who said she was thirty-two years of age and had never walked in her life, they heard me say, "Jesus heals you; rise and walk". They saw the young woman leap to her feet and run around the church. They all stood to their feet and many shouted Hallelujah, others clapped their hands, and they must have thought that I had come to this ministry very easily, that I was very used to it, and that I was very confident in it, and that I had in some way always done it. But this was very far from the truth. I came into this ministry by a very difficult path, and I needed a lot of convincing before I first laid hands on a sick person. In fact, as you will see, it needed an angelic visitation to assure me that this ministry was of God, and that I was to be engaged in it.

My encounter with divine healing ministry had begun many years ago when I was a young Methodist minister. I was walking away from my church, having taken a service at Clifton Methodist Church near Brighouse, Yorkshire, walking down the hill with a woman who had attended the service, and I had always thought rather strange in her appearance, looks and voice. She was talking to me about divine healing which I was loth to discuss. She said that her sister had just been diagnosed with cancer of the breast and that she had persuaded her sister not to have any medical treatment, but to rely solely on Jesus Christ to heal her and that medical assistance would only interfere with God's work. I eventually saw this woman die a terrible death, and I was determined to have nothing to do with divine healing ministry.

Next, there was an occasion when I went with Anne to attend a healing service at Bridge Street Pentecostal Church in Leeds. The church was packed, obviously with many sick people. A lady next to me said, "I suffer from diabetes and I have not had any injections for some days because I am relying on God to heal me today at this service". She went up for ministry, came back to her seat, collapsed, and was eventually taken to hospital in a coma. I determined to have nothing to do with divine healing ministry.

Then a third discouragement was when a young man I knew was suffering with terminal cancer and in great pain. I saw his wife was pulling his capsules apart, tipping out the contents of the crystals, putting the capsules back together again and giving it to her husband. I asked her why she was doing this because the tablets were pain killers of great strength, but she said, "I want Jesus to be seen as the only one involved in healing my husband". I eventually saw him die in terrible pain and I decided again never to have anything to do with divine healing ministry. However, the strong conviction that I held was eventually overcome by, dare I say it, the Lord Himself.

My whole concept of the Christian Gospel's message and ministry was totally revolutionised on May 10th 1969, at about 9.00 pm. I was alone at the house my wife and I bought at 40 Deer Park, Harlow, in Essex. I was engaged in a full-time teaching ministry at a school, as I had been very frustrated in my parochial church ministry and attempts to reach people with the gospel of Jesus Christ. I am sure, from what I have heard that in the churches and parishes where I ministered up till 1969, I had done some good by visiting and preaching in the usual parochial ministry. But for me it was far from what I had expected when I was converted from atheism to Christianity at the age of nineteen when I was suffering from a very severe and long-lasting emotional illness with panic attacks, phobias, anxiety and depression, living a life filled with fear and terror. Through my conversion I was actually healed of this mental problem in a very short period of time. Having had long periods off school and work I was now functioning without mental issues and this was a tremendous relief as Jesus Christ himself, and my knowledge that I had found of Him, seemed to be the healing factor.

However, after feeling being called to the ministry of the church in full-time service, a calling that was ratified first by my Methodist minister and

22

deaconess, and then by the Church of England committees, Bishop and so on, I engaged in parochial ministry for a number of years, but felt frustrated by the fact that I was unable to reach people outside the church in any real way with the Gospel message of Christianity in which I firmly believed. I went into teaching in 1967 as head of Religious Education at Passmore's Comprehensive School in Harlow, having obtained a London University Bachelor of Divinity degree and a Birmingham University Master of Arts (Theology) degree. So I was well equipped for this particular post in the school. I also helped in the church in the centre of Harlow, called St Paul's, as a part-time assistant to the Rev Donald Knight, and I found there a fruitful ministry in teaching Christians and discussing the faith, but still unable to reach those who were, as it were, outside the church, and as far as I knew not practicing or believing in the Christian faith.

However, on that night in 1969, I had previously spent two weeks in fasting and prayer for a real effective Christian ministry to those Jesus described as 'lost sheep'. I had heard of Pentecostal churches during my Christian pilgrimage, but felt that they were emotionally unstable and theologically unsound and would have nothing to do with them, relying more on my intellect and learning than on anything of the power of the Holy Spirit which they said that they had received. Anne, however, had gone to a Pentecostal church at Welwyn Garden City to seek help for her brother who was dying of cancer. He was called George, and I felt that I had little to offer him except a place in a rest home, or in a place where he could die in peace. That was all I could do for him. Anne, however, heard that a man called Peter Scothern was visiting Welwyn Garden City Full Gospel Church and had a healing ministry. So she went, taking one of our twin daughters with her. I would not go. She came back three hours later, having travelled by bus, full of stories for me, all healing miracles and other spiritual gifts like prophecy that had been exercised in the church. My curiosity, because of my own deep need, was aroused, so I decided to go with her one evening and saw for myself the power of the Holy Spirit at work through this man ministering to the sick.

This led me to feel that I too must seek some power and some way of effectively ministering to the sick. So I gave myself this period of fasting and prayer. I was so desperate to receive something of what I had seen of the power of God that I would willingly have tried to drink the Thames River dry of water if I could partake of this great blessing from God.

After this period of fasting and prayer, with no tangible feelings or results in my life and ministry at St Paul's Church, Harlow, I was very desperate to hear from God anything He wanted to say to me if indeed He ever did speak directly to anyone. So, at 40 Deer Park, on May 10th, 1969, I happened to be alone in the house. Our four children were in bed and asleep and Anne had gone out to visit a friend.

I realised that I could spend two hours at least, in prayer before going to bed with Anne, and so I got on my knees and begged God to bless my seemingly devoid Christian life and ministry.

At about nine o'clock that evening, as I was praying, suddenly I was aware that the room in which I was praying, the largest room in the house, the sitting room, was suddenly filled with the brightest light I had ever experienced. It dazzled my eyes so that I could hardly see. The brightness was brighter than even the sun could produce if I looked into it. As I knelt there, suddenly I felt I had to simply praise God our heavenly Father through Jesus Christ my Saviour. As I was praying and praising aloud suddenly my tongue went crazy, I lost control of it, and found myself speaking in what I recognised from the Pentecostal church as the gift of tongues. I didn't understand what I was saying to God but I felt my whole being was tremendously uplifted, especially spiritually. I stood to my feet with my arms raised towards Heaven and then I looked around. In the corner of the room I saw a huge white figure like that of a human being. This figure was so large that his feet were on the floor of the room and his head touched the ceiling and he glistened with a bright white robe around him. I did not know what this was about, but then he spoke in rather a rumbling kind of voice and said simply, "You are called to heal the sick," and then as suddenly as it had appeared the light became absolutely normal and what I took to be a divine figure, perhaps an angel, disappeared. As I stood there, suddenly Anne came into the room from her visit to the friend. She looked at me with amazement on her face and said, "Where have you been?" I said, "I don't know what happened to me, it's too marvellous, wonderful to try even to describe in ordinary words." She looked carefully at me and said, "Trevor, your face is shining like an electric light bulb; it's glistening with a bright light glow." I told her that I thought I had become a Pentecostal Anglican and shared with her that I felt that by His divine grace, and despite all my failings, despite all my frustrations and despite all my giving up on parochial ministry, God who had healed me when I was nineteen had carried me all the time on my way, as I was always faithful in my devotions, and always hard working in my churches, and diligent in preparing my sermons. Now something wonderfully different I realised was to be a very real part of my ministry in and from the Church. In a marvellous way, God had called me to heal the sick.

Chapter 3

The call to cast out demons

The existence of evil spirits, demons, unclean spirits, and such spiritual entities as existed without particular names but which could affect human beings in their bodies and in their minds, was taken for granted in the time of Jesus. Their existence in fact was never ever questioned. They were seen to be part of Satan's evil kingdom to test and try human beings and to war against all that was good and healthy in human life. Satan seems to have been the sort of head of this kingdom of darkness as he was himself regarded as a fallen spirit, and he was in charge of his attacks on human beings in many ways.

Jesus was once called Beelzebub, the king of the demons, by the Scribes and Pharisees when He was told He was casting out evil spirits by Himself being a very powerful force of evil in the world. Paul, in his epistle to the Ephesians, put this sort of satanic kingdom in this way, he said that we (Christians) wrestle not against flesh and blood but against principalities and powers, against evil forces of wickedness in high places, whom he said Christians should resist steadfastly in the face. The Greek words here can be rightly paraphrased as 'we are wrestling against beings without bodies' so they cannot actually be seen in themselves, but can affect human beings, especially as they seek to indwell human being's bodies and minds, and cause evil sicknesses and results to come about by their own particular spiritual power. In the New Testament, in the Gospels, we see that they can cause epilepsy, they can cause deafness, and cause a person to be dumb, they can also cause the spine to be bent and very painful, and they can also cause human minds to be very deranged or as we would say 'insane', shouting and acting sometimes with peculiar strength beyond what was humanly possible. So Jesus sent His disciples out on their first mission to extend His Kingdom, and He commanded them, as we have seen, to preach the Gospel, heal the sick and cast out demons. We read that the disciples came back from their mission full of joy and happiness saying to Jesus "Even the demons are subject to us in your name".

Jesus was not the only rabbi to cast out demons in the New Testament; He said on one occasion, "If you tell me I cast out demons by the prince of the demons, by whom do your sons cast them out?" indicating that other, what we would call exorcists, were going about doing this work. What the crowds found astonishing about Jesus casting out demons was the particular authority, very powerful, confident authority with which He Himself cast out demons. The crowds marvelled and asked 'who is this man to whom the demons are subject in this way?' Jesus also taught that casting out evil spirits was only the first part of a person's cure from whatever illness or derangement the demon had caused. He said that if the human life is not filled by other good powerful spirits, for example the Holy Spirit, demons may go away and then come back, find the house - in other words the human being - which they had left, very nicely cleaned, fresh and garnished, and bring in seven other evil spirits more evil than themselves and stronger than themselves, so that the last condition of the person who had been exorcised is worse than the first.

This belief in demons and evil spirits seemed to die something of a death over the ensuing centuries of the existence of the church. But it has not in any way completely died out even in our technological and scientific age. People will still go to séances hoping that some medium, by spiritual power and insight can contact the dead, or themselves now without bodies, or that people with spiritual power, not necessarily Christian, can heal people by what is called spiritual healing. Superstitions about good luck and bad luck, good spirits, good forces working for a person, still exist in our time as people engage in all sorts of occult practices like séances and Ouija boards, and even looking at the position of tea leaves in tea cups, and feel that still, even in our scientific age, human lives and circumstances can be very much affected by the existence of spirits, entities that cannot be seen. There are in existence people who are called black witches and white witches, who have their particular ways of meeting, casting spirits upon people, from the white witches for good results, black witches for curses and bad results. The power of curses is still very much believed in, and gypsies and so on are seen to have this power of insight into spiritual realms, and still today people will seek those who seem to have spiritual power to banish evil from their lives.

A very common belief that has persisted to our day is the belief in haunted places or haunted houses, and often spiritualist mediums, or sometimes hopefully Christian ministers, are called to a house where the occupants feel that very strange things are happening; banging and all sorts of odd things going on that cannot be explained in human or natural terms. So it's still practiced today. Occupants of what they believe to be haunted houses, sometimes castles, will call upon mediums to exorcise these places, usually of people who have lived in these places and usually have died there, which still inhabit their homes. The Christian church has, despite the decline over the centuries, of a belief in evil spirits since the days of Jesus, still believed in exorcism and still had exorcist clergy specially trained to deal with demons by exorcism, and ministers called upon to exorcise haunted houses.

In His day, Jesus gave His disciples authority and power to cast out evil spirits in His name, His name being regarded as a powerful spiritual entity denoting His presence and power, and they found that in His name they could be effective in this ministry. A case in point, seeing the disciples, after the death resurrection and ascension of Jesus, casting out evil spirits is found in the Acts the Apostles chapter 8 where Philip is on a mission, a

Christian mission in Samaria, and it is recorded that he healed many people who were lame and demons came out of people, the Greek word meaning screaming as they came. So this casting out of spirits was seen as an essential part of the early Christian's mission in continuing the work of their Lord Jesus Christ.

Now I myself had in no way, in my liberal days, embraced the reality of evil spirits. I thought that it was all superstition to be disregarded by intellectual and trained Christian ministers and that it was only, at best, a call back to the times of the Middle Ages when demons and exorcists were prevalent in human society. So I considered in my ministry, having served as a traditional minister, first a Methodist then Anglican in Brighouse, Todmorden, Barnsley, Halifax and Harlow, on no occasion did I have any consciousness or even a thought of any reality of demonic entities. I certainly believed that people should be born again and brought into the Kingdom of God, but I did not feel that in so doing they were being set free from evil spirits. However, it is important to note the old Christian renunciation that had to take place at baptisms and be recited by every candidate for baptism before they were baptised even up to our present times. They had to say, "I renounce the devil and all his works, the vain pomp and glory of the world and the evil desires of the flesh so that I will not follow or be led by them". They were baptised, and in the act of baptism they were commissioned to be Christian soldiers fighting against powers of darkness unto the end of their lives or the end of the world.

I eventually, in 1970, having had this momentous experience of the 10th May 1969, went to be vicar of the parish of St Paul's Hainault, where in fact everything manifested or portrayed in New Testament times was seen to be re-enacted in our ordinary parish church and its vicar – me – especially on Tuesday evenings. So I preached the Gospel, healed the sick, and never had a thought about casting out demons, although I saw it was an integral part of Jesus' commission to His church.

This all altered on one Sunday evening at an ordinary regular liturgical evening prayer service in my church of St Paul's. I had taken evensong in its liturgical way to the Nunc Dimittis 'Now let us, thy servants, depart in peace according to thy word for mine eyes have seen they salvation'. I was still in my robes at the end of the service, when a woman walked in through the end door of the church, went to the table where our Bibles were stored, and began to tear up the church Bibles, including the ones with hard backs, with phenomenal strength, and fling the paper and the books in the air. This had never happened in a church I'd had before so I left my pulpit and marched down the centre aisle and said to this woman, "What are you doing?" She turned around, faced me with seemingly glazed eyes and said in a strange voice, "I have come to destroy you before you destroy many of me". Then she marched towards me with her hands in such a position showing that she intended to strangle me. I knew I was not popular with all my parishioners but this was taking it a bit far! She marched steadily towards me; I went steadily backwards. She came to very near the chancel steps. 'What can I do?' I thought, then I suddenly knew what I should do not from any training or liturgy, there had been no such teaching about demons in my pastoral theology, but I knew what to do from New Testament reading. So I said, "Stand still! In the name of Jesus!" She stood rooted to the spot, she could not move forward, backwards or sideways. So I thought 'that's better, I seem to be in command', so I then did the next thing which came into my mind, I shouted, I don't know where this word came from except from the Holy Spirit, I said, "Witchcraft get out of her in the name of Jesus!" She let out a great scream that rang around the church, and fell on the floor motionless.

The congregation were horrified, they had never seen anything like this in church and their hair was pretty well standing on end with shock. I then knelt over this lady and laid my hands on her head and asked that peace would fill her mind and body, and the Holy Spirit would dwell in her. Eventually she got to her feet. She said "My name is Olive Allen, I have been a witch for many years and I have tried to get free of it but I've not been able to do so, and no one has been able to set me free. But now this man (me) in this church has set me entirely free. Now I will for the rest of my life serve the Lord Jesus Christ."

Olive became a wonderful dedicated Christian in our church and often told her story at my request in many churches and even on radio, and especially in detail on television, and brought peace and health to many people and hope. However it had a different affect for me. I felt shaken by this experience, a little devoid of energy, and after that every Tuesday evening for three or four years, until I left St Paul's Hainault in 1980, people used to come to the service to be set free of their demons which they felt they really had indwelling within them by this remarkable vicar Trevor Dearing – me – who eventually was dubbed 'England's Exorcist' because I had so much to do with this ministry, not by choice but being pushed into it as it were by the Lord, and in this strange way being called to do something in which I had never believed.

I remember going into Burnley to conduct an ordinary Christian mission and the lamp posts were decorated with placards saying 'Exorcist arrives in town'. That was me. In a way I felt sorry about this because preaching the Gospel was my primary aim together with healing the sick, but unfortunately this business of exorcism, because of a terrible event of a mistaken exorcism event in Barnsley in Yorkshire which filled the newspapers, exorcism was top line news and I was a top line minister to be asked by newspapers, radio and television to describe and engage in this ministry. Trevor Dearing, the ordinary Anglican clergyman who had never done anything spectacular in his life, and didn't even want to, was suddenly England's

Exorcist. The exorcist vicar, called by Jesus, I believe sort of pushed into it as a calling, to cast out demons and so fulfil the whole commission, on every occasion I went to other churches or took meetings in my own church, especially our Tuesday evening meetings, when people came from all over England by coaches and even from as far away as Singapore to see this remarkable scene of the New Testament in every aspect. Preaching the Gospel, healing the sick, demons screaming as they came, Acts of the Apostles re-enacted, shown to be a true ministry, shown in the Bible to be true in the late 1970s. I was called to cast out demons.

PART TWO

Called and Equipped

Chapter 4

Receiving the power

So we have seen, in Matthew chapter 10, that Jesus sent His disciples on what we may call a pilot or even trial mission to preach the Gospel, cast out demons and heal the sick. We have seen that they came back with at least some good report in so far as they had been able to cast out demons at least in Jesus' name. It seems that Jesus was pleased about this but He warned them not to put too much emphasis on it, but to realise that the most important thing was that their names were written in Heaven. So we go on through the Gospels with Jesus teaching, preaching, healing, and casting out demons, until it reaches His last time with His disciples in an upper room – the time of the Passover - when Jesus had told them He would be betrayed into the hands of sinners, be put to death – crucified.

In John's Gospel, there is a very full account of Jesus talking and teaching His disciples at that very important time. If we knew a particular evening was to be our last evening alive with those we loved, we would certainly regard it as very important indeed and be very precise in what we said to our loved ones, especially about their future and in any kind of relationship with what we had taught them. Jesus tells them He is going away and so it would be natural for them to think that because Jesus is going away all signs and wonders, healings and so on, would stop because He who could do all these things would no longer be on Earth. However, Jesus did not in any way indicate that this would happen, in fact, He said it would be the beginning of their real work for Him. He even said:

> "The works that I do shall you do also and greater works than these shall you do because I go to the Father."[13]

Jesus promised them that that they would not be left without any help when He went away because what He called 'The Comforter'[14] would come and be with them and even in them. The Greek word 'paráklētos' does not really mean comforter in the sense we envisage comfort, it really means someone who is sent to help, and is better translated for us a divine helper.

So Jesus went to His crucifixion, being completely in charge the whole way through, even choosing the moment when He would yield up His spirit and deliberately die for us. He rose again from the dead by the power of God, and Luke records that He appeared to His disciples for forty days. During this time, He made another promise to them about the Holy Spirit; He said that the Holy Spirit would be sent upon them to, as He said, "baptise them in the Holy Spirit"[15]. This means they would be totally immersed in the Holy Spirit, for that is what the word baptise in the Greek really means. He also said that when they were so baptised in the Holy Spirit they would receive power; He said, "You will receive power when the Holy Spirit is come upon you"[16]. The word 'power' in the Greek, 'dunamis', means an energy power in comparison to say the word meaning power by reason of one's status, which really is better translated as 'you will receive authority'. It was not this authority He was talking about which eventually they discovered they had later in their ministry; it was His power, in His name. It was energy – a supernatural energy power with which they would be filled and therefore equipped to obey Jesus' commands to extend His Kingdom, make disciples of all nations and do His work in a supernatural way.

In the days in which we live, the word 'power' is an important word. It is very often used for what we need to live our lives fully in this scientific and technological age. Human beings, I think, really first discovered a sort of power that was no longer dependent on human energy to do things, when they discovered coal. They found that this could be a source of power so great as even to drive Robert Stevenson's great locomotive trains with great weight behind them. Also it was used to generate electricity, another energy power that would be seen in say the lighting up of millions of light bulbs – electric lights in homes all over the country. They also discovered gas as a source of power and indeed we are even seeing in these days energy power through the splitting of the atom in atomic energy stations built around England, America and Europe; nuclear power. So the aim of human endeavour has been to increase, as much as we can, the energy power that is at the disposal of human beings; to energise all sorts of things for the wellbeing of human beings, of human life. In these days it has been a race to try and produce this energy with the lowest possible carbon emissions, carbon being seen to cause what is called 'global warming'. So we see energy not so much as it is being transmitted but in the results that it achieves.

Jesus was called by John the Baptist, when He appeared before him to begin His ministry, the man on whom the Holy Spirit would rest. Jesus began His mission using supernatural energy power, which had come upon Him in the form of a dove, to work all kinds of miracles, healing in Nazareth, Galilee and beyond. Jesus had 'dunamis' from which we get our word dynamite – supernatural energy power that effected marvellous miracles of healing, and even miracles that did not involve healing like turning water into wine, feeding five thousand with five barley loaves and two small fish, walking on water, and producing a great mass of fish when none were there. In fact His power seemed to be quite limitless, especially when He raised a man called Lazarus from the dead when he had been dead for four days[17].

So Jesus called His disciples to a great mission to preach the Gospel, heal the sick and cast out demons. But they were just ordinary men, fishermen, tax collectors, a terrorist, in no way seemingly qualified to undertake this vital work for Jesus and indeed for humanity. Jesus had promised them that they would do greater works than His, and He had promised them after the Resurrection the supernatural energy power with which to do it.

It was on the feast of Pentecost, the first day of the week, when the disciples, numbering about one hundred and twenty followers of Jesus, were gathered together in an upper locked room for fear of the Jews, all with one accord and one mind, and all at prayer. It was then that the result of this supernatural energy power was seen. It was felt in the form of a 'mighty rushing wind' and seen in flames of fire resting on each of them[18]. So the wind spoke of a corporate experience which they would all have, belonging together in Jesus' service and name, and the fire of an individual experience of the power of God which they would receive because it rested upon each of them.

As we have seen, energy power is seen mainly by the results which it achieves which are often beyond what has been previously anticipated. In the case of the Apostles, it is recorded that the supernatural energy power was seen and resulted in them speaking in tongues, languages which they had not learned, languages of nations into which they had not been or been in any way initiated in their language. It is recorded in Acts of the Apostles that the crowds heard them speaking in their own languages, in all the different languages from which the people had come, in which they heard the disciples speaking[19]. So the Apostles had received not only a call but now a supernatural equipment of energy power with which to fulfil the Lord's command. It has been argued by some, known as 'dispensationalists', that this particular energy power and its manifestation in speaking in tongues, healing, and so on was just for that period of time before the Apostles had all died, after which it would never more be seen to be used or even needed. However, there is nothing in New Testament writing to indicate that this was to be the case. There is no indication that this was not to be continued until the Lord returned in glory. Certainly 'speaking in tongues' went out of fashion for some centuries, but was rediscovered by some Christians meeting in America at a place called Azusa Street, California, when suddenly they began to speak in tongues. Eventually this spread, not only amongst these people who called themselves 'Pentecostals', but also through what's been called the 'Charismatic Movement', even being seen and used in traditional denominations like the Episcopal Church of America and eventually in the Church of England and other denominations in England.

So it was that I had been called quite definitely to this three-fold ministry of Jesus, and I have related this to show that this need was still wanted by Christians who obeyed the Lord's command, even in the twentieth century and in an ordinary Church of England minister, myself, because on the 10th of May, 1969, I was not only called to heal but for the first time I spoke in tongues, prayed aloud in tongues, and sang in the Spirit. I had been seeking, as I have related, this power in my own life and now I had received it and was, I felt, an ordinary man being supernaturally endowed by the Lord Jesus Christ in the Holy Spirit; baptised in the Holy Spirit, so that I, an ordinary man, with a lot of problems in his early years, not even liking religion at all, not liking Christianity and being ill and physically weak, eventually ordained as a Church of England clergyman, I was now endowed by Jesus Christ Himself with the Holy Spirit with which I could begin to fulfil His command and see the results of this energy in an ordinary church with what had been an ordinary minister. I had received the power, I had been supernaturally endowed.

Chapter 5

The power of the name

We have seen that Jesus was equipping His Apostles who go out on their mission, obeying His command to preach the Gospel, heal the sick, and cast out demons, and that He was not sending them out in a powerless way or just as ordinary human beings; He was sending them out with supernatural equipment for their task. He had, as we saw in the last chapter, promised and actually endowed them with supernatural power 'dunamis' with which they would be able to accomplish great miracles, and we also now see that He sent them out with another form of power. This power consisted (in our English word) of authority. These two forms of power represent two Greek words 'dunamis' – supernatural energy power, and now 'exousia' – power being operated, in fact achieving its result, by means of the status of the person.

At the beginning of His ministry, He was known as Jesus of Nazareth, and later, after the resurrection, when He spoke to Paul, He referred to Himself as Jesus of Nazareth[20]. When He came to the point of equipping His disciples for their task, He said, in effect, 'you can use my name, Jesus, Jesus of Nazareth, to effect great miracles, healings and deliverance from demons'[21]. He said there would be power in the use of His name. I regard this as a sort of giving of a power-of-attorney by Jesus. In our day, the power of attorney means that a wealthy powerful man, probably very rich, can tell certain people whom he trusts that they can have the power of attorney to allocate, spend, and use not their own resources but the resources of the person named. So Jesus said 'use my name' to the disciples, 'and with my name I give you the power of attorney, all the authority to use all my resources, my spiritual resources, to effect great miracles and other matters which I want to be done for my Kingdom'. So we read in Matthew's Gospel that He said "If two or three are gathered together in my name, they can ask what they will and my Father will grant it from Heaven"[22]. It was not what they had as disciples, but now they were using Jesus' resources given to them by the use of His name to effect great results. He said on another occasion that "when two or three are gathered together in my name, I am there in the midst"[23]. I believe this is the simplest definition of what we might call a 'church' in the New Testament; Jesus' presence with two of His believers, followers, to do His work. So "whatsoever you ask in my name, I will do it that the Father may be glorified in the Son"[24]. He said you may ask for whatever you want in my name and it will be yours for the furtherance my Kingdom and the blessing of you and my people.

We have seen that in an earlier mission, the disciples came back to Jesus saying 'even the demons are subject to us in *Your name'*. So a precursor to the fact that on a larger mission, wider mission, that name would bring victory over all evil forces; there would be power in the name of Jesus. We see in the Acts of the Apostles, power by which people could be saved from their sins in Chapter 2, also power by which people could be healed. On his first preaching mission to the assembled Jews at Pentecost, Peter healed a sick man and said 'It's Jesus, it's the power of His name it's faith in His name which has made this man sound in the presence of you all'[25].

In a later mission, Philip is seen to be preaching the Gospel in Samaria and healing sick people, and it is recorded that he cast out demons that screamed as they left the people they inhabited[26]. So Philip was engaged on a one-man obedience to Jesus' commission to preach the Gospel, heal the sick, and cast out demons. This mission went on and in the Acts of the Apostles we find that Jesus, who it is said, had ascended the place of highest authority in Heaven at the Father's right hand, now gave His Apostles the right to use all the authority and power He had in Heaven to effect the work of His Kingdom, bringing glory to His name, and by using that name, attesting to the fact that "this Jesus whom you crucified is both Lord and Christ"[27]. So the disciples carried on their mission to preach in the first sermons they did at Pentecost in the streets of Jerusalem and around using the divine energy power and using the divine authority power to bring about the healing of a man who had been lame since birth, sitting at the Beautiful Gate of the Temple. He came into the Temple, it is said, "walking and leaping and praising God"[28]. This was because Peter had used the energy power to heal this man's legs, and the authority power of Jesus to get him to walk and make him completely whole. So the Apostles went on in their mission, using Jesus' name.

We must see however, that the use of the name of Jesus cannot be used as a sort of mentor or a sort of magical slogan to effect spiritual realities. Yes Peter had said it is in His name that this man was healed, that we receive forgiveness for our sins, His name - the name of Jesus. But it is not just saying 'Oh I'm sorry Jesus', we have to really believe in Jesus; be fully surrendered to Jesus as I have previously described; abandoned to Jesus, really believing in Jesus. We see that while casting out demons from Olive Allen, described earlier, I didn't know what to do. As soon as I used the name Jesus, saying "come out of her in Jesus' name", they came out; the witchcraft came out of her.

And so I continued bringing people deliverance not through my own authority or power but using the authority of the name of Jesus. Similarly, when we utter prayers and say 'we ask these through Jesus Christ our Lord' we are not going to get answered prayer unless we are confident in that name we are using, not using it just as a form of words, but really confident that Jesus Christ will answer this prayer in the name of Jesus we say.

So Jesus left us not only a powerful gift in energy power, but the right to use His name to achieve victories in every realm of spirituality. There is power in the name of Jesus to deliver, and the name of Jesus has set captives free. The power of the name of Jesus has set alcoholics free for instance or anybody in bondage, and in all this we are saying this is a matter of the risen ascended Christ at work, and it is His Kingdom we are extending, using His name as a witness to His resurrection, ascension, and abiding glory.

Chapter 6

The power of prayer

Prayer is a factor in the lives and in the being of all major religions in the world. Whatever the religion, believers in it do spend time in prayer both privately and corporately. Prayer is a very major factor in the lives of believers who are Christians. We are not concerned that other religions or its believers also embark on prayer, for Christians it is not a matter of whether we pray or not, but to whom we pray and what we pray about is of vast importance. Christian prayer can best be summarised as speaking aloud or in one's mind and heart to God the Father who, as it is stated in Genesis, created Heaven and Earth; it is to Him, God, Creator and Father, who we pray in the name of Jesus Christ and in the power of the Holy Spirit.

So we see that the founder of Christianity, Jesus Christ Himself, set aside time to pray despite His heavy workload in His ministry on foot, going about all over Samaria and Galilee, all over the Holy Land as we know it, teaching people who would listen to Him in great crowds about the Kingdom of God, which we shall discuss in the next section of this work; despite that intense effort and activity and energy of Jesus, not only teaching people these truths but also, we are told, as He was followed by great multitudes of people who listened to Him, He also spent a lot of time in healing their sick and infirm and also casting out any demonic powers that were in their lives. We believe His ministry lasted only three years, but in that time He did a phenomenal amount of teaching of religion, of Christianity, that changed the whole world from the beginning of His time to the present. So Jesus, despite His tremendous activity, we are told in the Gospels, spent a lot of time in prayer to His Father no doubt. We are told that often a great time before day He went aside into a solitary lonely place, and in the silence of that place He prayed to His Father, and no doubt that was a tremendous source of His spiritual power and strength, a tremendous direction as to where He should go and minister next, in the next day; He would receive guidance from His Father about His teaching and about His travelling.

Jesus also taught His disciples to pray as a very important part of their lives, especially their spiritual lives. He was asked by them to teach them how to pray and so He taught them what we know as 'The Lord's Prayer', beginning 'Our Father which art in Heaven'[29], which we believe has been a prayer uttered by Christians from the time of Jesus to the present time. It is in fact a model prayer containing everything important that a Christian ought to pray about.

Jesus thus continued His ministry and taught and healed and cast out demons for about three years, going eventually to Jerusalem where He had foretold that He would be handed over to sinners, to gentiles, and be crucified and by the power of His Father rise again on the third day. His disciples were told to pray that their faith would not fail at that vital time. They prayed in the Garden of Gethsemane while Jesus went what is called a stone's throw away from them, and prayed alone the most important prayer of His whole life and ministry. He prayed we are told with such earnestness and depth that He sweat, as it were, great drops of blood[30].

When He had risen from the dead, He appeared to His disciples we are told for forty days and then He told them, before He ascended into Heaven in their sight, to go to Jerusalem and wait for what He had promised would come, as we have seen, the power of the Holy Spirit. So it was as they were gathered together, it is recorded of one accord, in one place, of one mind, praying earnestly to Jesus as He had taught them, that day received the power of the Holy Spirit; a mighty rushing wind and tongues of fire. So what we can envisage as the first great beginning for Christians of their work of spreading the Kingdom of God's message over the whole world, making disciples of all nations, began in prayer, for it was as they prayed that they received, as we have seen, the power to do what Jesus had commanded them to do in His name.

It is recorded in the Acts of the Apostles that the practice of prayer was very much a part of their being together for worship and fellowship "they met together for prayer, for fellowship, for the Apostle's teaching and prayer"[31]. So it was that prayer was an important part of any Christianity and has remained the same to the present day. So when, for instance, Peter was cast into prison, facing possible death, the Christians did not go about with great placards saying 'set Peter free', or with great protest marches, they in fact prayed him out. So Peter, about midnight in prison, found his chains fell off, the guards fell asleep, the prison doors were opened and he went out into the open air in the street. It is recorded that he could hardly believe himself what had happened to him, and when he arrived at the house and the room where the Christians were who were praying for his release, and knocked at the door of the house and it was answered by a maid called Rhoda who declared 'Peter is here', and it is probably a good thing for us who often fail in our faith, that it is recorded that they could not even believe that they had received the answer to their prayer, believed that what Rhoda had seen was not Peter but a ghost[32].

Christians on their mission, as recorded in Acts, spent time together in prayer. It is notable that when they were sending Paul out on his first missionary journey, that they did so after prayer and after laying their hands upon him, commissioning him for his ministry.

As we go on from the Acts of the Apostles, we find in the Book of Revelation that it was in prayer on the first day of the week that John the Divine was met by the risen, ascended, and glorified Christ. So we see all the time in the church's history and ministry, the importance of prayer, as we have seen either individually in The Lord's Prayer for instance, or corporately as in the room where they received the Holy Spirit.

In the history of the church, we see that prayer was continually used, sometimes developing into what we call liturgies, or patterns of prayer, that Christians could pray together, for instance when they met for the Lord's Supper, or in seeking a substitute Apostle to take the place of Judas who had committed suicide after betraying Jesus. In my own ministry, prayer was always an important part of every day's activity and it was while I was in prayer myself, on the 10th of May 1969 that I had this wonderful experience of the presence of an angel and my call to the ministry.

During my time as a minister of religion in the Church of England, I used the Prayer Book for Common Worship and my own prayers as I was instructed and promised to do. It was very important for me, as my ministry suddenly exploded at St Paul's Hainault, with vast crowds gathering to meet for the Gospel Healing Service and to hear me preach, that I spent all the day before that meeting, especially on a Tuesday, in prayer before walking out of my vicar's vestry, standing in front of hundreds of people and beginning to engage in ministry. It was with prayer that I, and those helping me minister to the sick, praying for healing for them to the Father in the name of Jesus and by the power of the Holy Spirit, and seeing so many of them healed, and we also prayed for the power of the Holy Spirit to descend upon the assembled congregation which He always did as they burst into singing in the Spirit and praying in tongues.

As I went on my world-wide mission of Power, Praise, and Healing, eventually with my wife Anne, we always insisted that there was a great time of prayer before we began any Christian meeting. The practice of getting up very early in the morning for two or three hours personal individual prayer has been my practice right up to this time in my eighty-sixth year.

It is a sad fact that as I have travelled around various churches, of all denominations, that I have found prayer to be often the missing factor in the life of nearly every church I have missioned in, and I am sure this is a reason why in mission generally, quite apart from when I was there, Christians have found a very poor response and a very slow, if at all, building up of their Christian congregation. At a church where I worship there is only a prayer meeting once a month for half an hour before a morning service and it is usually attended by the same half-a-dozen devout church members. Just for illustration, on another occasion when I was taking a meeting in the large Pentecostal church in Birmingham and a great crowd was there waiting to hear the message of the Gospel, my wife Anne went down to join the prayer meeting below the church in a room underneath the church; she went there and found there was only one other person besides herself, praying for God's blessing and the mighty power of His Holy Spirit to be upon the meeting that I was about to take. Why has this happened, maybe because of some disillusionment in not receiving answers to prayer, or because it takes a lot of discipline and time to engage properly in the practice of prayer. I am sure that the church, especially in Europe and western society, is so weak today and so often sees very little in the way of conversions of unbelievers to Christ, because the habit of prayer, or rather the practice of prayer, is being so sadly neglected. We have seen in the Acts of the Apostles, and I saw in St Paul's Hainault, that prayer is not just a matter of words; it is a source of tremendous spiritual power. I am sure it was such a necessity for Jesus even as the Son of God, for Him to pray to receive power to heal, to preach and cast out demons in His own wonderful ministry.

"Why do we need to pray?" asked one Christian of me, "when God knows, as it is recorded, what we need before we ask". I am sure that the answer lies in the fact that in prayer we are, as Paul says "co-workers with God"[33]. Although He is sovereign and He is almighty, He has set this limit upon Himself to need us to preach the Gospel so that people may be healed, and for us to cast out demons so that they may be freed of evil spirits, and to bring healing to the sick in our day, because it is as we pray that power will allow, an invisible spiritual power, to effect what we are praying about as it ascends to the Father and descends to the person or area, to bring about change and wonderful spiritual results in those for whom we pray. So I am sure that as Jesus commanded us to preach the Gospel, heal the sick, and cast out demons, He was assuming also, before we ever attempted to do this, either individually or corporately at any time, we would embark, if possible with as many other Christians as we could find, in prayer, for there is power in prayer.

PART THREE

Thy kingdom come

Chapter 7

Preaching the Gospel

In the first part of this book I shared how I was called by God to preach after having been a young atheist, convinced atheist, and disliking anything religious, not believing a thing about God or anything to do with religion, and in fact disliking it intensely. I shared that I was called to preach and it was in fact a call to preach the Gospel because Jesus has said 'preach the Gospel' and I was seeking to obey that command.

What is meant by the word 'Gospel'? The word means, in English, 'good news'. So I was to preach good news to those who listened to my messages or sermons. This was to be a very positive subject to preach about and as is further elucidated by Jesus, because in Mark's Gospel it says He came to preach the good news of the "Kingdom of God"[34]. So the Kingdom of God was what Jesus came to announce as now having arrived "the Kingdom of God is upon you"[35] said Jesus - it is here and now, fact. In Matthew's Gospel it is called "the Kingdom of Heaven"[36] but reading Matthew's Gospel we see that it is really the same thing as the Kingdom of God.

What then is a kingdom? A kingdom in everyday language or common parlance is as a certain earthly piece or section, large or small, usually large land; a kingdom is really what we would say of a country in its own right and it would be ruled by a king who would determine its laws, determine its justice and organise its whole life. To be a member of that kingdom, to be a citizen of that kingdom, was to be one who would obey the established king in every way. So where is this particular land that God is to rule? The ruler of it, in Scripture, is called "The Messiah" meaning an Anointed One or The Anointed One[37]. It was a supernatural term to denote that the King Himself would not only be human but would have supernatural powers at His disposal to establish and maintain His rule.

This was very much what the Jewish people at the time of Jesus really thought about the nature of a kingdom. To them, their land consisting mainly of Galilee, Judea and Samaria, was the land that David had occupied as the ideal king in his time centuries before Jesus. So the king in Jewish thought at the time was one who would come from Heaven with supernatural powers and abilities to put-to-flight the Romans, and end the Roman Empire and its rule over the Holy Land that was considered to be God's country, and the Messiah would rule in place of the Romans, having completely routed them in battle. This view was hard set in the minds of Jewish people at the time of Jesus, so we see His disciples asking Him is it at this time you are going to restore the kingdom to Israel? Jesus' reply was "It is not for you to know times or seasons which the Father has fixed by His own hand"[38]. Only He knows when this will be established and what nature it will have. So the Kingdom in Jesus' understanding and teaching was not this Earthly kingdom of Jewish rule with the Messiah reigning from Jerusalem. In His thoughts, the Kingdom was essentially spiritual in nature, for He said "The Kingdom of God is within you"[39]. He told Pilate that His Kingdom was not of this world because if it was His servants would fight. When He was condemned to death by Pilate, He was mocked, given a crown of thorns upon His head, a sort of reed as a weapon in His hand, and a royal robe around Him. So Peter beheld His arrest and his mind would have gone back to that time on the road to Caesarea Philippi when Jesus asked His disciples, "Who do men say that I am?" and Peter replied on behalf of them all "Thou art the Christ (Messiah), the Son of the living God"[40]. It was at this time that Jesus began to teach that He would be betrayed into the hands of sinners and put to death, crucified, and with his conception of his contemporary Jews, Peter could not see this happen to the Messiah and told Jesus "this shall never happen unto you"[41]. Jesus replied "Peter, get behind me Satan for you do not understand, you only understand Earthly things and not Heavenly things about God's Kingdom"[42].

Jesus had this message of the Kingdom almost entirely in His teaching. He told many parables about the Kingdom of God and started talking in this way: "The Kingdom of God is like..." then came the parable. In every case it was not the kingdom the Jews of Jesus' time envisaged would come by the power of the Messiah. So as we study the nature of this Kingdom, not being of this world, we see that it is in fact spiritual reality or a spiritual Kingdom. It is the Kingdom of God, the rule of God in human hearts which have repented of their sins and given themselves in obedience utterly to God and His rule. That is why Jesus would say obedience is better than sacrifice. The Father wanted in His Kingdom those who would obey Him utterly and entirely, and live to spread around all over, indeed the world in the end, this fact of the rule of God in human hearts.

So the Gospel is good news. It is good news about something very specific; good news about a Kingdom, the Kingdom of God, because now it was at hand, here, it has come in reality. So I was called to preach not my own thoughts or ideas or my own philosophy or theology; I was called to preach specifically very good news to my congregations; the news that the Kingdom of God was here now in this scientific and technological age, and that it was a fact to be believed and to be entered into, bringing with it not only life in this world but eventually life in what the Bible calls Heaven.

As I listened to other preachers, I heard them speaking to me and to others. Their concept of the Gospel was that 'you are all sinners and by God's judgement of you, you are doomed, dashed, and bound for hell'. They went on to say that the only way out of this dilemma was to accept the fact that Jesus (the name means saviour) had sacrificed

Himself to God, who was the only one who could meet the justice of God because He was completely without sin, and by His willing sacrifice was able to pay the price of human sin. The traditional Gospel that they then proclaimed, was that every individual sinner to blame should accept Jesus as their personal saviour and then live a Christian life in relation to God until they died, and having been 'saved' would certainly go to heaven.

They taught, quite rightly, that no man could earn his salvation by any amount of being religious, or by doing good works, say of charity. This was based especially on Paul's letter to the Ephesians 2:8. It was also based on what Jesus said, that "He who called Himself Son of Man came not to be served but to serve, and give His life a ransom for many"[43]. This teaching sought to be absolutely right as far as it went, but it missed out the all-important fact that Jesus had said that His basic and ultimate mission was to establish the Kingdom of God on Earth. So He taught us to pray "Thy Kingdom come, Thy will be done, on earth as it is in Heaven"[44]. This kingdom was to consist of so many people whom John talked about in the Book of Revelation, so many eventually, out of every nation, kindred and tongue, worshipping in Heaven the glorified Jesus; the Lamb that had been slain.

This message of the Kingdom of God is absolutely paramount to understanding the New Testament. This Kingdom could be entered here and now[45]. Saved believers entered into a new relationship with

62

God – a very close relationship – to be actually experienced; a new purpose for living and a new hope in dying. He taught that this Kingdom would fully come at a time which He Himself could not predict; when He Himself would judge every individual of mankind by what they had done[46]. Jesus therefore did not come to start a church, especially as we know it now – as an institution. The Greek word for church itself does not mean an institution or buildings, but refers to a kingdom of people as 'the called out ones'. This was the Gospel I was 'called to preach' - good news for mankind – for which I have preached in many different ways to this present time.

Chapter 8

Healing the sick

In 1969 the angelic figure said to me "You are called to heal the sick". He knew that I had always prayed for sick people in their absence, in intercessory prayer; I had done what most minsters always do. However, I envisaged and saw, and was taught by the Holy Spirit that the command to heal the sick involved more than intercessory prayer for sick people. I say again, I had been called, although I had never done it, and was very nervous about doing it, and didn't know how to do it, and even though I had the faith to do it, I had been called to do more than intercessory prayer, I was called to what I have described as a divine healing ministry to the sick in their presence, and I have seen great glory to the Lord through me; imperfect vehicle though I am for God's grace to flow.

Of course, not everybody is healed. I regard my ministry as doing the best I possibly can, with the best faith I know how, and after much time in prayer as obedience to God and the angelic call I received. I do it in obedience and will continue to be obedient to my death's day. When asked, I will not precursor the ministry by going out of my way to suggest the person receives healing and going around hospitals for instance to get the sick out of bed. The person must ask and seek, that is the beginning of the ministry. But I have done it the best way I can. People are not healed all the time, sometimes, although it's hard to say it, through lack of faith. We remember that Jesus could do no mighty works in Nazareth because of their unbelief, their lack of faith; because they knew Him so well as a carpenter's son. We read that Jesus always commended people's faith. "Your faith has made you well," He said to a woman who said not 'If I could but touch the hem of His garment, I *may* be healed,' no, nor 'if I touch the hem of His garment *perhaps* I shall be healed,' no. "If I touch the hem of His garment," she said "I shall be healed,"[47] and to another woman, Jesus said "Great is your faith, let it be done to you according to your faith."[48] I am not saying I always have perfect faith. I am not saying that I accuse people – that would be very bad – of not having faith. No, they know and I know that I will do my very best in ministry, and the issue in the end is God's work not mine, because I cannot heal anybody myself, not even myself.

It is interesting to note that not everybody was healed in the New Testament record. The great Apostle Paul, who healed so many people, had to say "Trophimus I left ill at Miletus"[49] and "Epaphroditus was sick unto death but the Lord had mercy on him,"[50] and he told Timothy to "take a little wine for your stomach's sake and for your frequent infirmities"[51]. Paul himself had what he described as a 'thorn in the flesh', something in his body that was hurting him and impeding him in his ministry[52]. It is noted however that he underwent tremendous experiences of persecution, being ship wrecked and so on; he must have been tough. But he besought the Lord, he said, three times that this angel of Satan sent to buffet him, that God would take it away. But God apparently said to him "No I won't for my grace is made perfect in your weakness"[53]. "For when you are weak," said Paul, "then you are strong"[54].

I am sure some people are not healed who would have been healed if Jesus had been there, obviously, because He was a perfect channel of the Holy Spirit's work in divine healing. He didn't always use the same words twice in His healing ministry; to every individual He spoke different words. However, I have to say some people aren't healed because, although I try my best, and after much prayer and a prayer life to bring God's healing to people, I am not a perfect instrument in any way through which this channel of healing can flow; certainly not as Jesus was. However, we must engage in this ministry of healing in obedience to Jesus' divine command as an integral part of beginning to establish His Kingdom here on Earth and eventually in Heaven.

We preach and we carry on preaching, not because everybody we preach to who is not a Christian is converted, they are not, we know that, but we do it in obedience to God because that is what He has called us to do in helping to build up His Kingdom. Of course since Jesus' day, medical science has made dramatic steps in the alleviation of pain and suffering and the healing of sick people, and

Christians do not in any way disdain this wonderful work in any way; they pray that it will continue and improve and blossom forth and we believe God uses it in many, many ways to heal sick people. Often it is not a matter of 'do I receive my medication or divine healing?' it is both; receive your medication 'and divine healing as well', through the prayer of faith for the sick. People even have to have faith in the medicine they are receiving or the operation that will be performed. So we support medical science with our prayers and believe it is part of God's work, even His greater works to bring in His Kingdom more perfectly on Earth as people are healed.

However, the vast majority of people who have sought healing ministry from me have not been healed by medicine in any way. Maybe their condition has been somewhat alleviated but they still are in desperate need. So we see healing taking place by God, not only when medical science is not used or cannot work for the person. We see divine healing in many cases in relation to what is happening with the person medically. So I share with cancer patients that they should receive chemotherapy, nasty as it is, or radiation therapy, temporary as it is, as part of the work of God for their healing. However, I say that they should also receive divine healing ministry as well for we are not bothered about proving anything - as Jesus wasn't - about God and His power. We have compassion on sick people and want them to be healed, with the help if possible of medicine or surgery, and also divine healing. We often bring about healing where doctors have given up on it happening, or far more quickly than doctors have envisaged, often completely reversing medical prognosis, to give the glory to God and thank Him for His healing work as we preach the Gospel, and heal the sick, and as we shall see, cast out demons as an integral whole of His commission to the Church as He seeks to establish His Kingdom on Earth and in Heaven.

Chapter 9

Casting out demons

People, even Christians, reading the last chapter about divine healing may still think, sadly wrongly, that this part of Jesus' ministry, or his commission to heal the sick as part of the work and manifestation of His Kingdom and of His own 'Messiahship' can be jettisoned and put on one side in Christian practice as being mainly unimportant in contrast to preaching the Christian Gospel. I hope I have vindicated the ministry and shown it to be really important, in fact vitally important for the expression of the Kingdom of God being manifest on Earth.

When it comes to the casting out of demons, if Christians thought divine healing was somewhat irrelevant, as in church practice they seem to be doing, casting out of evil spirits, perhaps we could say they would want to put in the spiritual dustbin. Certainly I didn't study this ministry or feel in any way I was called to do it – deliverance or what is commonly called exorcism – in my own ministry ever, and as I shared with you in previous chapters, I was pushed into this ministry, probably against my will by God Himself. So I would describe myself at that time as the reluctant exorcist.

What we must really see about this ministry is that yes, it is very important for the deliverance of people who are tormented or in any way afflicted, as we have seen even in their bodies, by demons or unclean spirits. It is indeed important that someone living in the Holy Spirit, or ministering in the Holy Spirit, should have the gift of discernment also, which is promised in 1 Corinthians chapter 12[55]. Not so that we can discern that a person is, as we say 'possessed' by unclean spirits, the Greek for that does not occur in the New Testament. What does occur is that a person can be 'demonised', that is the real meaning of the Greek word. So when a discerning minister like me sees that being 'demonised' is really the basic problem in a person's life, even when they may be showing signs of emotional or mental afflictions and problems, mental issues, we still need to have at our disposal the ministry of deliverance, and see people, as I have over many years, really set free, body, mind and spirit by the power of Jesus' name.

This ministry is not about the energy power, 'dunamis'; this ministry involves knowing that Jesus is not only risen but is ascended into Heaven, sitting at the right hand of God, "Far above all principalities and powers and every name that can be named not only in this world but in the next"[56]. So, as I have often preached, it is the power of Jesus' name and the authority given to Christians to use that name - in Greek 'exousia' - that must be used to set people free, as I shared in my story earlier about my being used by God to bring deliverance to Olive Allen. It is when I used the name of Jesus with authority, that I had no doubt of the inevitable result that was so important. Demons have spoken to me from 'demonised' people and said, "not afraid of you," and I have replied, "No, you're not afraid of me but I come to you," addressing the demons, not the person, "I come to you in the name of the Lord Jesus Christ," and several times demons have in fact replied to me, using the voice of a woman, slightly different, and have said, "we are frightened of Jesus". We have seen in the New Testament that demons pleaded with Jesus, saying, "do not cast us out before the time".

I feel that this particular subject must be dealt with as I am now sharing within the context of the whole message of the Kingdom of God. This particular ministry is a manifestation of the power, authority, of Christians within the Kingdom of God, as seen in the account of Jesus in the Gospels, casting out evil spirits in a dramatic, and to the people of the time, incredible way, using His authority. They accused Him, the Pharisees and Sadducees, of casting out demons by the prince of demons named Beelzebub. Jesus replied that "a kingdom divided against itself could not stand"[57]. So He said "If I, by the finger of God cast out demons, then know that the Kingdom of God has come upon you"[58]. In that sentence alone we see that this particular ministry is closely related, in fact intertwined with the message of the Kingdom of God which we are in this book discussing.

When Jesus said "the Kingdom of God is at hand,"[59] what He was saying in fact was that not only is the Kingdom of God a matter of fact here and now in me, and in my proclamation of God's power and authority, He is bringing this whole matter of the victory of God down to Earth. He is saying that the Kingdom of God is now here, yes, but He is saying that the Kingdom of God is now being manifested on the Earth. Religions, especially Christianity, have been sort of insulted by people saying it's all about 'pie in the sky when you die'. However, we are seeing, especially in the ministry of divine healing, and now even more in the ministry of casting out of demons, in Christianity, the power of Jesus to bring it about, God's Kingdom; not just a cosmic event, but a matter of fact here on Earth, here and now.

What this ministry is indicating and definitely saying is absolutely true, is that within the Kingdom of God, Christians have victory over all evil, following the fact that Jesus Himself had victory over all evil and that in the Kingdom of God and its manifestation, evil is completely defeated. Yes, Jesus met this mainly as an evil force, in the power of Satan's kingdom - his messengers and disturbers of human life and causes of often sickness and torment and distress; he met it in demons and unclean spirits. But in the fact that He Himself, and also the Disciples who he sent out on their mission and who came back saying "even the demons are subject to us in thy name"[60], we are seeing that Jesus is completely victorious over all evil forces, because He could cast out this form of evil, Satan's demons, disturbing and tormenting human life. They had no chance against the authority of the Messiah, Jesus, and His Kingdom, and even no power at all, only weakness when Christians – ordinary men, came at them using the name of Jesus, seeing them defeated in His name.

This indicates that there is warfare going on, not only in Heaven, but on Earth, between the sheer goodness of Jesus and His Kingdom and the forces of evil under the authority of Satan, 'the adversary'.

We see that in the casting out of demons we are fulfilling and answering some of the prayers Jesus told us to pray when He said "Thy Kingdom come, Thy will be done, on Earth as it is in Heaven"[61]. In the casting out of demons, God's will is being done on Earth as it is in Heaven, although there is still a great deal to do to mop up all these evil forces that have been defeated by the death, resurrection, and ascension of Jesus the Messiah.

We see in the Gospels that even as Jesus was set to embark on this mission to humanity of bringing in His Kingdom as it was now and on Earth, Satan tried very hard to set Jesus away from this goal in His mission to give His lot in and to give His power in with the kingdom of Satan which the New Testament is very clear to expound and expose. When Jesus was about to embark on His mission, we read in the Gospels that He went into the desert to fast, in a remarkable way, from food and drink, and to pray, and it seems to get direction from God about how He was to set about His work, and guidance from God His Father about His ministry and His mission on Earth. However, His prayers for the direction He had to take in bringing the Kingdom of God to Earth was interrupted by Satan (Greek 'satanas' meaning adversary), who said to Jesus that if He, Jesus, would throw in His lot with him, Satan, he, Satan, would give Him all the kingdoms of the Earth[62]. Jesus of course rejected completely this temptation as He knew His life and ministry, death, resurrection and ascension were the path that He should take. So we read that Jesus got rid of Satan's temptations by quoting the Word of God to him "God has said". We read that Satan left Him at that time, to come back at a more convenient time.

We read also that when Jesus was told by Peter, in Jesus words by revelation of the Father, that He Jesus, was the Christ, the Son of the Living God, it was then that Jesus began to say for the first time that He must suffer and die, and as we have seen this was not the concept which the Jews had at the time of the Messiah, and certainly not what Peter thought would happen when he confessed Jesus as the Messiah, the Christ. Jesus' reply is significant; He said "Get thee behind me Satan"[63]. So He saw that through even Peter, who would be the rock on which Jesus said He would build His Church, Satan could speak and tempt even the Messiah away from His path of death on the cross as a sacrifice. We read also that as Jesus was in the last days before His arrest, He said when Peter said he would never deny Him, "Peter, Satan demanded to have you, to sift you as wheat, but I have prayed for you that your faith will not fail; and when you have triumphed, strengthen your brethren"[64]. So we see on Earth, at this vital time, the initiation of the Kingdom of God by Jesus; the work and existence of the powers of terrible evil in the cosmos, and on Earth. Even Christians tend to forget that the problems of humanity, wars and rumours of wars, and even the present pestilence called the 'COVID 19' virus, are the work of evil, initiated in the end by Satan himself.

So Christians, from the very outset, even at their conversion, are enlisted by Jesus in warfare against the powers of evil. "Soldiers of Christ arise and put your armour on," says the old hymn, "strong in the strength which God supplies through His eternal Son". We read of this cosmic battle between the forces of good in Jesus' Kingdom and the forces of evil in Satan's. This is mentioned in several passages in the New Testament, for instance, "Be careful; be vigilant, for your adversary the devil, prowls around like a roaring lion seeking whom he may devour. Resist him, steadfast in the faith"[65]. Paul in Ephesians chapter 6 says "For we wrestle not against flesh and blood, but against the principalities, against the powers, against the world rulers of this present darkness, against the spiritual hosts of wickedness in the heavenly places. Therefore put on the whole armour of God."[66] We read, however, that when He ascended to Heaven, Jesus "led a host of captives, and He gave gifts to men"[67]. The picture here is of the triumphal procession which the victorious Roman generals led through the streets of Rome after they had succeeded in conquest of another nation, trailing behind them the rulers of that nation and many of their spoils, to the cries of triumph from the assembled population.

So we see in the New Testament that Satan is only spoken of as a real and terrible power afflicting mankind with many diseases, and tormenting the minds of many people. We see that he is, through the initiation of the Kingdom of God through Jesus at that moment and on Earth, completely and absolutely defeated, and his end, as thrown into the lake of fire, is not in doubt. So we see the casting out of evil spirits by Jesus and if Jesus' diagnosis had been incorrect the person would not have been healed. It has been the same in my ministry when people have been cured through deliverance ministry; I know that my discernment and diagnosis of the person's condition has been completely right and inspired by the Holy Spirit.

This ministry, I was reluctant to engage in, because of its demands upon my life and my spiritual inspiration and endowment, and which has always left me feeling much more exhausted than preaching the Gospel or healing the sick; I was reluctant to undertake this ministry. One Bishop even told me he didn't believe demons ever existed, and certainly not now. However, I told him that Jesus, who I had spoken of in the creed as, "God of God, Light of Light and Very God of Very God," believed in demons and cast them out as evil forces, so did the Bishop mind if I believed Jesus rather than him. He was not pleased with my reply in that way. Christians today take the same attitude as that Bishop, towards demons, but, as I say, it was a very important part of Jesus' ministry, that's why He commissioned the Disciples to continue it. This is because, in bringing in His Kingdom and His mission to do so amongst people of His time in the Holy Land, Jesus constantly met the forces of evil in the evil spirits that were as it were Satan's angels inhabiting human lives. We see, in His complete victory over these evil forces in human life, His victory, not only over all evil forces on Earth, but also in Heaven. The destruction of all the powers of evil by the forces of the Kingdom of God, especially Jesus Himself, is thus pre-empted.

To come to my own ministry, and what I have advocated with others, is that we do not go about our Christian work actually looking for demons. I have met Christians who are too demon-minded to really be of any use to Jesus. One woman who I knew for instance was frightened of spiders, so fellow Christians tried to cast out of her the demon of the fear of spiders; this demon is not named in the New Testament. It happened that when they said the ministry was now complete and she was freed, a spider ran across the floor in front of her and she screamed blue murder. So their diagnosis and discernment had been far from correct. Some Christians, perhaps rarely these days, are too much involved and thinking about ministering about demons. However, it is the neglect of this ministry that invalidates a very vital issue in Jesus' ministry in the Kingdom of God.

In fact, in my ministry, I have not looked for demons, but I have found that, as in the New Testament, even in the ministry of Jesus, that I have been preaching, or when I have been laying hands on the sick, demons have manifested themselves, sometimes with screams and blasphemy and all sorts of ways which are obviously seen as evil; it is then that I have used the name of Jesus to cast them out and see the person, as one said to me, "I have been tormented for years; now I am at peace in my mind". It would be dangerous to regard all mental illness or problems like neurosis and psychosis as demon-initiated, and to think that the person can be cured by deliverance ministry, known as exorcism. Thankfully, I have studied psychology, the psychology of religion and abnormal psychology, up to degree standard and that has helped me a lot, but in the end it has been spiritual discernment to decide when a person, say tormented in their mind, is actually demonised. I have sometimes thought that such a person would be easily cured of their mental torment, or psychosis, if it was a matter of their being demonised; they would soon be set free by the power of the name of Jesus. However, I will share that I have also had to engage in deep counselling ministry with some people to get to the root of their problem lying elsewhere than in demons, before they can be healed. I have written about my experience in this ministry of healing of the mind in my book that I have called 'God and Healing of the Mind', which I know has been accepted as sound from a psychiatric point of view, and has brought much help and healing to Christians through a spiritual point of view. When people seek counselling from me, I say if you are looking for a secular answer please see a secular psychiatrist; only let me minister to you if you are seeking what I will offer you, that is, spiritual answers, scriptural answers to your problem.

One of my most wonderful ministries in the healing of the mind has been with my daughter Rachel who lives now in Seattle. Through no fault of her own, she suffered a major nervous breakdown that made her very ill. She consulted a prominent psychiatrist and had lots of medication – all to no avail. I was distressed by her suffering especially when she called me on the phone. However, when she phoned me one evening I said to her, "do you think your dad can help you?" "Yes," she replied eagerly. I began to counsel her on the phone and she has become so much better. She is now a mature Christian, a leader in the four-thousand-strong church to which she and her husband belong. She said that the telephone conversation changed her life and was the most important suggestion I ever made in her whole life.

As I write this, I know that what I say will come as a shock to some Christians, but I have to say that when Jesus said to His Disciples, "Preach the

Gospel, heal the sick and then cast out demons"[68], He was not just being imitative of the thoughts and ideas of His own age. He was declaring that through His Kingdom coming here on Earth, the Kingdom of God, His Disciples in their mission could see the victory in this Kingdom over the forces of darkness and evil as they cast out demons. Even then Jesus had to say "Do not be so joyous in this, but rather that your names are written in Heaven"[69]. That is what I feel He has said to me when my deliverance ministry has been advertised on lamp posts as 'the exorcist vicar is in town'. This has brought me into trouble with my own church, and one Bishop in particular just now prohibiting me from being invited to preach in the whole of his Diocese in the Church of England.

Thankfully, the Pentecostals embrace me and ask me to mission there in their churches. But I am an Anglican by ordination, and like John Wesley I will say "I live and die a member of the Church of England". But I do not rejoice that in deliverance ministry I have seen Jesus' victory, in bringing the Kingdom of God right down to Earth, over evil forces that really expresses what is happening in the cosmic order in the heavens; I know that I must not rejoice in this where I have seen constantly people freed and never ever seen a failure in using the name of Jesus in the deliverance ministry where it has been necessary. I have heard His voice saying, "Do not rejoice in this Trevor, that the demons are subject unto you, but rejoice that your name is written in Heaven."

PART FOUR

The Kingdom of God

Chapter 10

The Kingdom grows and expands

We have seen that Jesus left His disciples having endowed them with power from on high, and said that they must be witnesses, especially to His resurrection, in Jerusalem and Samaria and to the uttermost parts of the Earth. The divine messengers at the Ascension indicated to the disciples that they would not see Jesus return in any like manner as He had now gone until He would come to finalise the whole of His work and mission. So they returned to Jerusalem, received the divine energy power and authority power, and set about their work for the Kingdom of God.

It must be remembered that Jesus had once told a parable about the Kingdom of God, saying that it was like a mustard seed sown in the earth[70]. This seed He denoted was the smallest and least of all seeds that would ever grow, so tiny it would be almost unrecognisable. However, He said that once this has grown in the earth it would bear fruit, and would produce leaves and fruit a hundred fold, and it would be like a large bush so that the birds of the air would be able to come and lodge in its branches. So Jesus told His disciples not to disdain small beginnings but to see that this principle of growth, in the hands of God, like the mustard seed would produce this large bush, the Kingdom, and the birds of the air would come and lodge in its branches.

The Acts of the Apostles records the wonderful work that the disciples did. Although a relatively inconspicuous and motley band chosen by Jesus, they had received His supernatural anointing for their work, and as we read through the Acts of the Apostles, we see that they do indeed set about doing their work all over the then Holy Land, indeed in Jerusalem, Judea, Samaria and to the uttermost parts of the Earth. We do not see this in any relatively planned or coherent way of doing it; we see that individual Apostles were used by God in remarkable ways to do His work and to bring in His Kingdom.

So we see Stephen preaching a long sermon about the Kingdom of God and challenging the Jewish leaders about their constant historical rejection of the prophets and messengers sent by God. He was eventually stoned to death and it is noted that the lynch party laid their clothes at the feet of a man named Saul, who of course we meet later on[71].

We see the same principles at work in the mission of the Apostles as they obeyed Jesus' command in the Gospel account of Him sending out His disciples to do their missionary work. Once again, we note that they preached the Gospel - as we have seen Stephen did, healed the sick, and cast out demons.

We first meet Peter doing this on the day of Pentecost in Jerusalem as he had gone to the temple with John at the hour of prayer and had been used by the Holy Spirit and the Name of Jesus to heal a man who had been born lame from birth and who everybody knew was a complete cripple[72]. This miracle of healing, again in line with Jesus' instructions about healing being a very real part of His message and ministry, brought hundreds of people to the Apostles, asking how this had been done by these ordinary men, and Peter was able to point to the fact that it was the risen Christ, it was His Name, used in 'exousia' power, that brought this man, he said to the crowd, his perfect soundness in the presence of you all. So Peter pointed from a miracle of healing, to the reality of the Messiahship of Jesus and the fact that although the Jews had rejected Him and crucified Him, He was now being honoured by God the Father as Lord and Christ. So right at the beginning healing is part of the Christian message and gives place to it being preached.

Moving on we see that Peter continued to be used in what I have called divine healing, and that on every occasion this presented a possibility for preaching about the Messiahship of Jesus whom the Jews had rejected. We read that the people brought the sick into the streets of Jerusalem that even the shadow of Peter might pass over the sick people, and as many as the shadow passed over were completely healed[73]. This is a special miracle of divine healing, again in the Name of Jesus. We read also that aprons and handkerchiefs were taken from sick people to the persons of the Apostles and that the people who received them back were remarkably healed and that, again remembering the maxim of Jesus in His teaching about proclamation of the Kingdom, many people had evil spirits go out of them as well[74].

This theme of healing, preaching, and casting out of evil spirits, continues throughout the whole of the ministry of the Acts of the Apostles and is an obedient act following Jesus' command. It still had the authority of Jesus, His blessing and His power and brought about the expansion and growth of His Kingdom.

Again we see this in the ministry of Philip in Samaria, in Acts chapter 8, where he conducts a sort of one-man revival in the Name of Jesus, and we read that the lame are healed in a remarkable way and we read also that demons came out of them, "screaming as they came"[75]. However, the Apostles had to come from Jerusalem to lay hands on these new converts because they had not yet received the Holy Spirit and it was believed that they could only do so through contact with the ministry of the Apostles.

We read also that this same Philip, enjoying a wonderful revival in Samaria, was, as it were divinely transported onto a desert road where there was no one there, and he must have wondered what he was doing there, but suddenly a man came along in a chariot, a eunuch who was the Chancellor of the Exchequer of the kingdom of Ethiopia. This meeting, this divine appointment, has all been organised by God. The Ethiopian is reading what we know as Isaiah chapter 53 about a man who was despised and made acquainted with grief and rejected and so on, and Philip joins the chariot. The Ethiopian asks Philip 'who is the man who is being spoken of by the prophet, himself or another', and so Philip is able to preach unto him Jesus. The Ethiopian eunuch says that he wants to be baptised to complete his conversion[76].

Eventually we move on to the conversion of Saul of Tarsus on the Damascus road, as he sees a wonderful vision of the risen Christ shining more brightly than the sun and he wonders what this means. The answer from the vision says, "I am Jesus who you are persecuting, arise and I will show you what you must suffer for my Name's sake"[77]. So Saul of Tarsus, now becoming Paul, received the laying on of hands by a man named Ananias, to receive back his sight and to "be filled with the Holy Spirit"[78], because even Paul could not minister in power without this endowment of energy power and authority power from on high.

So with Paul we see missionary journeys actually being planned to go into the Roman Empire to visit the main cities of the Empire, like Galatia and Philippi, to which Paul wrote letters after he had been there and nurtured them as young churches in the faith. Paul himself was used in miraculous acts of healing, again as Jesus had commanded. At Lystra he healed a man who was lame from birth and the people wanted to worship him and Paul had to tell them that he was not a god and again preached unto them Jesus.

A disturbance about the faith also occurred in Ephesus, Acts chapter 19, because the disciples Paul and Silas were saying that adultery was a sin and so disdaining the god precious to the Ephesians who they all worshipped.

We see all these persecutions breaking out against the Apostles as they held firmly to the faith. They usually preached firstly in the synagogues, declaring that Jesus, whom the Jews had rejected, was both Lord and Christ. Paul went about his missionary journeys with Barnabas and in the beginning Mark, accompanying him as they set about bringing the Gospel to the major cities of the Roman Empire, and Paul had a great vision and determination that his mission would not be complete until he had preached the Gospel in the capital city of the Empire, Rome itself. He arrived in Rome following a shipwreck, but again by the determinate plan and counsels of God it seems that he was quite a free man in Rome, to proclaim the Gospel and to write his letters to other churches.

So throughout the Acts of the Apostles we see the Kingdom growing and extending according to Jesus' parable about the mustard seed. We see God's purpose being planned and not hindered by anything man could do. We see the early Christians still obeying the three-fold command of Jesus to preach the Gospel, heal the sick and cast out demons, as an intertwining whole in their work of proclaiming the Kingdom. So it is relatively strange, given what I have recounted in the forgoing pages, that Bible-believing churches that preach the Gospel feel they can cast on one side as unimportant divine healing ministry and the casting out of evil spirits. But as the Bible has taught us, as Jesus has taught us, as the Acts of the Apostles has taught us, these are an integral three-part concept of one mission, one intertwined mission, and that we will only see the glories of Jesus, building His Kingdom on Earth, when all three facets of His Gospel are loyally adhered to and completely expounded.

Yes we may see all sorts of versions of Christianity, including feeding the hungry and tending the sick and getting known in neighbourhoods and doing all sorts of things which make them quite popular amongst people. Sometimes I have met churches that I think I could describe as spiritual cosy clubs as the challenge of the Gospel is really not uttered. But if we want to see the real work of the Kingdom in our day in a secular and evil society, we must not disdain Jesus' command to the Apostles in the Gospels for the furtherance of His work in the Kingdom in the Acts of the Apostles showing us exactly how mission today in the twenty-first century should be done, should be obeyed, and then when we do it altogether we will see the results we shall see.

So we have seen that Jesus gave a commission to His disciples to spread the message of the Kingdom of God and bid people enter it by repentance and faith to which he also added, in the conversation with Nicodemus[79], the necessity of the new birth.

We have seen that this commission was held faithfully and kept very faithfully too by the disciples in their missionary work in the time of Jesus' Gospel and then in the spread of the Gospel in the Acts of the Apostles.

We have been dealing with material and sayings and actions that were recorded in the Bible nearly two thousand years ago. So we must now ask, is this commission still relevant in this scientific and technological age of the twenty-first century? Or does it need reinterpreting in a dramatic way? Does it need modernising in the light of modern thought and investigation of religions and philosophies? We could assume that this might be so with such ancient material, were it not for the fact that even now in 2020 we have seen this maxim of Jesus at work and His Kingdom being built up wherever the Gospel is preached, the sick are healed, and demons are cast out. I would especially share with readers my own experience of an ordinary Anglican clergyman, called to preach, called to heal the sick and called to cast out demons in the year 1969. Did this message fall on deaf ears? Was it not properly understood? Did it need reinterpreting?

The answer is a definite no. It was as powerful at St Paul's Hainault, where we embarked on this three-fold commission of the Gospel, as it was in the days of Jesus and the Apostles. But now this maxim, this proclamation, this endowment, this promise was given to be fulfilled by a very ordinary Anglican clergyman in whose ministry nothing spectacular in any way had happened but who felt called to these three-fold ministries in ways I have described, and I set about with my heart and soul in them, to fulfil them.

You will see at once that I was not simply called to a preaching ministry in which I had engaged for a number of years with partial success. I had now been commissioned to the ministry of healing which was its counterpart and, as it were, partner in salvation. I also saw that demons were still present in the world in the twentieth century in human lives, and indeed in the whole force of evil in the world, so we needed to deal with them as well.

So in some trepidation and fear, I laid my hands on a lady called Carol who was suffering from a mental illness. She was regarded as incurable. I laid hands on her, the best way I knew how, in faith, and she immediately declared that she had been healed and shared her healing through prayer for rightful sanity with the local newspaper. So it was not my preaching of particular quality or dynamic that drew the next largest congregation they had ever seen at St Paul's Hainault the following Tuesday to the meeting. It was not announced as a healing service either. It was announced as what we called a 'Power, Praise and Healing' service at which the Gospel would be preached and the sick would be ministered unto. So the first big crowd came on that Tuesday evening in September and healing miracles began to happen, and as I preached people came forward to accept Jesus as their Saviour, whether they were healed or not, and, as I have said in the case of Olive Allen, demons had to be cast out of at least one person.

This ministry at St Paul's Hainault continued on every Tuesday evening at 7.30. As the miracles began to be publicised, and talked about even on the relatively poor housing estate, people began to flock in to the church. There was a time of ecstatic praise with simple choruses, singing, clapping hands and raising arms and so on, the people were very happy. I preached for usually about half an hour on the Gospel message of the Kingdom of God in various facets of its meaning and then invited people to come forward to receive prayer for their salvation or their healing. Dozens of people began to flock forward down the aisles to myself and to some other clergy who I'd enlisted to minister with me. After laying hands on them my wife shepherded them through what we called the covered way into the church hall that was set out with tables and chairs with Christian literature, and were populated by very mature Christians, and my wife put people with mature Christians who she felt had experienced the same kind of need answered in their lives as was being described by the seeker.

So the healing ministry went on, many people falling to the ground under the power of the laying on of hands on their heads. We had several people catching sick people and laying them down so that they would not hurt themselves – although nobody ever did. There were cases of deliverance ministry, especially of a young woman named Denise who was an alcoholic who used her money, she said, to buy drink, and the money came from her prostituting her body so she could buy drink. This was a particularly fearsome deliverance ministry as the demon argued with me in words like, "Jesus is dead, I saw Him die". The ministry went on about twenty minutes before I felt sure she was completely delivered and then she was taken into the church hall and the next day she was interviewed by newspapers, declaring her complete freedom from evil spirits.

This sort of ministry went on and on at St Paul's Hainault; it was not exaggerated, we did not look for demons but any who were present would manifest themselves as the power of the Holy Spirit came upon the meeting and so we often had to minister deliverance almost as an emergency to people who were being tormented by these evil forces, and many, many, people during the next five years were set free from the powers of evil spirits at St Paul's Hainault. However, I must say that the number of people set free from evil spirits was very small in comparison to the many hundreds of people who made professions of faith, acknowledging Jesus as their Saviour and Lord, and entering the reality of His Kingdom.

The healing ministry went on, somewhat mixed up with the conversion ministry and the deliverance ministry, because people came forward not knowing what they were seeking and the Holy Spirit revealed their real need. There were so many miraculous healings at St Paul's Hainault that I could not for a moment begin to write about them because it would take several books. However, some people did write in their testimonies of healing to me and these were published in a book, written by my wife and myself, called 'The God of Miracles', where people gave their own descriptions of what had happened to them now they were healed. So we believed in total healing at St Paul's Hainault, healing of the body, mind, and spirit, within the realm of the Kingdom of God.

Emotional illnesses were also healed at St Paul's. One lady was pretty well dragged in, men holding her two legs and arms and she was screaming out in great terror and fear, and I anointed her with oil in the Name of the Lord. She became very calm and on television later, when asked how long it took for her mental condition to be healed, she said she had been in and out of psychiatric hospital four times and it took a long time, but at St Paul's Hainault, in my ministry she was healed in "half a minute".

Doctors, local and far away, brought their sick people to be ministered to at St Paul's Hainault, and many people who could not find their answers in medical science or psychiatry found their answer in what we called the ministry of Dr Jesus and no prescription charges necessary. So for three hours at least, the meetings went on and on, in praise and adoration for the risen Christ who two-thousand years ago had commissioned His disciples to preach the Gospel, heal the sick, and cast out demons. That commission has never changed, and has never lost its effect; St Paul's Hainault became a beacon of light in England, with people travelling from all over the country to find the Lord; the Lord who gave His command two-thousand years ago still at work in a little church with a failure of a minister.

PART FIVE

God's purpose realised

Chapter 11

The end times

We saw that at the beginning of His ministry, Jesus announced that the time was fulfilled and the Kingdom of God was at hand. In other words, in God's plan time had reached its optimum goal and the Kingdom of God was now being inaugurated by Jesus and it could be entered into now; you could become a member of God's Kingdom at this moment, through repentance and faith and through the new birth. We saw that Jesus proclaimed the advent of the Kingdom to be through the preaching of the Gospel, healing of the sick, and the casting out of demons, and this was fulfilled all the time in His own ministry and then in the ministry of the Apostles as recorded in the Acts of the Apostles.

Before Jesus was crucified however, on the night in which He was betrayed, the disciples began to ask Him a very definite but rather strange question. They asked when will these things come to pass, that is the destruction of the Temple, when will be the end of the age, when will be your coming again? Jesus replied that it was not for them to know the times, that God had His own purpose and that He, God the Father, was the only one who knew the precise time of the end of the age and when He, the Messiah Jesus, would come back again in glory; even He, Jesus, did not know that precise time. However, He began to tell them that although this time would be hidden from them, and indeed from Him, there would be what He called 'signs of the times'. There would be signs in other words that these things were about to take place for all who would heed these signs and understand them. He said they knew how to tell the times of seasons by looking at the sky and discerning that summer was near and yet they did not know how to read the signs of the times that Jesus would be returning in glory and the end of the age would have come.

So apparently the disciples, after Jesus' death and resurrection and the coming of the Holy Spirit, had to keep an eye open, as it were, for the 'signs of the times' that Jesus would soon be returning. Jesus prophesied that there would be wars and rumours of wars, earthquakes in many places, and pestilences, but the end would not be yet, but it would be, as it were, coming soon.

Jesus taught about this particular end of the age in parables about the Kingdom of God when He was declaring the nature and purpose of the Kingdom. He said that it would be as if a vine dresser, or rich man doing business, had gone away on a journey for a long time having left his servants very definite tasks to fulfil. The businessman would indeed come back and would hope to find that his servants had done very well with the money or talents he had given them and had traded them in such a way as to make a good profit. He warned them against being slothful in their business because his coming was delayed. So the master (Jesus, King of the

Kingdom) would return and mete out rewards and possible punishments for how the servants of his had been faithful to the task to which they had been committed. So this delay, in the coming of the master to his servants, and their not being slothful in their business but performing the tasks he had left them with faithfulness, is part of Jesus' teaching about the future of the Kingdom at the end of the age.

Jesus also forecast that some of His servants would, because of the delay in His return, become rather, as it were, slothful and would not be really looking out with expectation for the coming of the King of Kings. Because of the delay they would get rather haphazard in their dealings and lose their sense of expectancy for the return of the King of the Kingdom. Jesus warned His disciples, His servants, about this that would happen in His parables about the Kingdom. He reiterated this in His parable called the ten virgins. Five were wise and ready for the coming of the bridegroom and five were foolish and had not got any preparation of oil for their lamps, and then when the cry went forth 'The bridegroom cometh' they went out to meet him and the five wise virgins would be let in and the door would be shut, they would be in the festivities of the wedding, and the others would try to get in but could not because they had not been prepared and the door was shut. So this kind of teaching was given by Jesus in parables to His disciples about the finality of the Kingdom and the delay in His return after some long time. So Christians still need to heed the warnings of these parables.

Jesus also foretold that He would then be the judge of mankind and that mankind would be divided before Him like two different sorts of animals, sheep and goats, and the faithful ones, who had faithfully served the Kingdom in giving and tending to Jesus' needs or the needs of His disciples, would be welcomed into their eternal destination and rest, but the others would be thrown into outer darkness. So the definite facts about the future of the Kingdom are that the coming of the King to His Kingdom would be delayed and His servants must keep watching and waiting in expectancy, and also that the King of the Kingdom, Messiah, would come this time to judge mankind and welcome into His Kingdom those who have been faithful in their tasks and in their waiting and expectancy. These teachings of Jesus, in parables, about His Kingdom of the future were recorded in the Gospels and of course the disciples took note of them and were somewhat puzzled by the teaching.

So we turn to the teaching of people like Paul in his epistles about the end of time; the end of the age and the finality of the purpose of God bringing the fullness of His Kingdom. The events that would happen at the end of the age are portrayed by Paul in what is called 'the rapture' in 1Theselonians chapter 4, where he says the dead in Christ will rise first and those that are still alive will be caught up with them to meet with the Messiah in the air, in the clouds so they will be taken to be with the Lord. Paul's great chapter on the end time is recorded in 1 Corinthians chapter 15 where he says that the trumpet will sound and the dead shall be raised incorruptible and we shall all be changed. So Paul realises that at this end time death will be defeated, saying the last enemy that will be destroyed is death, and he says that Christians will rise from the dead with new kinds of bodies. Paul taught that there were different kinds of bodies like the moon and stars and earth and sun, but he saw that those who rose from the dead at the sound of the trumpet would meet the King, Messiah, in the fullness of His Kingdom; that they would have what he called incorruptible bodies that would never fade away and they would inherit the Kingdom with new eternal, everlasting, spiritual bodies. Perhaps he meant a body similar to the one Jesus had after His resurrection when He appeared to His Apostles for forty days.

The teaching goes on especially in the book of Revelation in visions recorded as being given to John the Divine on the Island of Patmos where he was being held as a sort of captive, although rather a free one, because of his faith. And John tells of a heavenly Kingdom and that there will have been a time of great tribulation on the Earth before this actually took place, for the persecution of Christians, especially by the devil, with the insignia 666 of which he will inscribe on the foreheads of those who decided to follow him. However, in Revelation chapter 7 we see this great picture of

144,000 Jewish people standing before the Throne and before the Lamb, with palms in their hands, and a great multitude which no man could number standing there with them praising the Lamb, 'glory honour praise and power be unto the Lamb forever'. And when John asked who these people dressed in white standing before the Throne were, he was given the reply 'these are those who have come out of the great tribulation and washed their robes and made them white in the blood of the Lamb, therefore they are before the Throne of God serving Him day and night in His Temple'.

The completion of the Kingdom, for those who have decided to follow Jesus, and those who have in their life time repented, believed and accepted Jesus as the Messiah, goes on because this new final phase of the Kingdom is seen to be one where John sees a new Heaven and a new Earth coming down from Heaven prepared as a bride adorned for her husband (marriage feast of the Lamb), possibly the bride being the Church, without spot or wrinkle, perfect in purity and in beauty and in love, to marry as it were the King of the Kingdom of God. John is told that in this new Heaven and new Earth God will dwell with men, He will be with them and be amongst them and be their God, and that there will be no sun to light this new kingdom in a new ethereal state of existence because the Lamb of God will be the light of the city of God; that there will be no more death (remembering Paul said in 1 Corinthians 15 'death would be swallowed up in victory'), no pain, no sickness, no death, God wiping all tears from their eyes and that nations will beat swords into plough shares and spears into pruning forks and they would not learn war any more.

So we see that in this wonderful vision of the Kingdom fully realised, John shows us the end of the age and the end of time and the very purpose for which Jesus came in the flesh announcing that the time is fulfilled the Kingdom of God was at hand, leading men to repent and believe the Gospel.

So we see that the theme of the Kingdom of God and the Messiah goes right through the New Testament, right through Matthew to the end of Revelation, and so those who are 'children of the Kingdom' have great hope for the future. Indeed they have a foretaste of the life in this Kingdom here and now (John 17 verse 3), but it is to be fully realised in the future, the end of the ages when the purpose of the Kingdom will have been completely fulfilled.

Bible References

---

[1] Matthew 10: 5-8
[2] Mark 6:7
[3] Luke 10:20
[4] Galatians 4:8-9
[5] Matthew 10:5-8
[6] Luke 4:33-36
[7] Mark 5:1-15
[8] Matthew 10:1
[9] Mathew 11:30
[10] Joshua 7
[11] John 19:30
[12] Philippians 2
[13] John14:12
[14] John 14:26
[15] Luke 3:16
[16] Acts of the Apostles 1:8
[17] John 11:17
[18] Acts of the Apostles 2:1-3
[19] Acts of the Apostles 2:6
[20] Acts of the Apostles 22:8
[21] John 14:13-14
[22] Matthew 18:19
[23] Matthew 18:20
[24] John 14:13
[25] Acts of the Apostles 3:16
[26] Acts of the Apostles 8:7
[27] Acts of the Apostles 2:36
[28] Acts of the Apostles 3:8
[29] Matthew 6:9-13
[30] Luke 22:44
[31] Acts of the Apostles 2:42
[32] Acts of the Apostles 12:6-12
[33] 1 Corinthians 3:9
[34] Mark 1:15
[35] Matthew 12:28
[36] Matthew 4:17
[37] Daniel 9:24-27
[38] Acts of the Apostles 1:7
[39] Luke 17:21

[40] Matthew 16:16
[41] Matthew 16:22
[42] Matthew 16:23
[43] Matthew 20:28
[44] Luke 11:2
[45] Luke 17:21
[46] Matthew 25:31-46
[47] Matthew 9:21
[48] Matthew 15:28
[49] 2 Timothy 4:20
[50] Philippians 2:27
[51] 1 Timothy 5:23
[52] 2 Corinthians 12:7
[53] 2 Corinthians 12:9
[54] 2 Corinthians 12:10
[55] 1 Corinthians 12:10
[56] Ephesians 1:21
[57] Mark 3:24
[58] Luke 11:20
[59] Matthew 4:17
[60] Luke 10:17
[61] Matthew 6:10
[62] Matthew 4:8-9
[63] Matthew 16:23
[64] Luke 23:31-32
[65] 1 Peter 5:8
[66] Ephesians 6:11
[67] Ephesians 4:8
[68] Matthew 10:7-8
[69] Luke 10:20
[70] Matthew 13:31-32
[71] Acts of the Apostles 7:54-8:2
[72] Acts of the Apostles 3:7-10
[73] Acts of the Apostles 5:15
[74] Acts of the Apostles 19:12
[75] Acts of the Apostles 8:5-7
[76] Acts of the Apostles 8:27-38
[77] Acts of the Apostles 9:5
[78] Acts of the Apostles 9:17
[79] John 3:1-15

Lightning Source UK Ltd.
Milton Keynes UK
UKHW040313280520
363924UK00002B/165